INDIGENOUS MANUAL FOR LIFE

INDIGENOUS MANUAL FOR LIFE

[LIFESTYLE FOR THE NEW AGE]

FIRST EDITION

BY BANDELE EL AMIN [COMPILED]

Indigenous Manual for Life, First Edition

ISBN-13: 978-1523418916

ISBN-10: 1523418915

Published by

CreateSpace Inc

Copyright 2016

TABLE OF CONTENTS

CHAPTER 1: INTRODUCTION

Now more than ever has the so called "Black's" of the diaspora need to reconnect to the creed of their ancestors. Enslavement of melaninated[1] humans over the past 600 years has created a detriment to society and a massive hole in the soul of the people. So much information, spiritual knowledge and culture were destroyed due to enslavement. This holocaust and genocide has effects directly related to the conditions of melaninated people in contemporary times. It is evident the Slave Trade created a beast of a person. The enslaved melaninated person lost his status as human. The enslaved, now has no political power. Without political power, the enslaved is deprived of their indigenous human rights. Human rights are the foundation of indigenous culture. Sovereignty is created through human rights. To be sovereign means to govern one's self. A sovereign body such as a state, tribe, or nation has the political power to protect the rights of the people. Protection of rights allows the people to create a culture that uplifts and benefits society. The enslaved melaninated human is not protected by law of the land

---

and therefore restricted from cultural development and political power. Human right violations among melaninated beings are prevalent today. We can look at Trayvon Martin, Mike Brown, Eric Garner and so many others in the recent past killed and denied human rights. In the case of many, no penalties nor punishment is ever received. Non melaninated police officers patrol highly melaninated areas with intent to use force. Racial profiling is prevalent.

Melaninated indigenous people today must deal with past enslavement by restoring their indigenous self. The lack of knowledge of self created the void which must be addressed. The void of self includes but not limited to spirituality, cultural identity and citizenship. It is very important for melaninated people to study their indigenous culture and incorporate into their lives. We live in the era of time where hidden information and knowledge is more available. The rise of internet has created a conscious community striving to learn more about themselves and their ancestors. This books deals with reclaiming culture and way of life. Many in the conscious community have come to the conclusion to change their way of life. Diet, marriage, raising children, education, religion and many other topics will be examined in this book. The key to this book is to examine the indigenous lifestyle and restore MAAT to melaninated minds.

CHAPTER 2:
MELANINATED INDIGENOUS CULTURES

The term "indigenous" is *adjective* originating or occurring naturally in a particular place; native. "the indigenous peoples of America". The conscious melaninated being is the indigenous person on the planet. Controversy exist among many scholars as to whether African's or dark skinned people inhabitant the Americas' first. The definition of American in 1928 was:

AMER'ICAN, a. Pertaining to America.

AMER'ICAN, n. A native of America; originally applied to the aboriginals, or copper-colored races, found here by the Europeans; but now applied to the descendants of Europeans born in America.[2]

The term copper colored is a peculiar word to describe Native Americans based on present day descriptions and portrayals. Let's look at indigenous people throughout the world, particularly America.

Evidence of melaninated remains around the world conclude that they were the first inhabitants in those regions. This is evident due to scientific research pointing to the origin of man coming from the Mother Land Africa.

Scientists have long held that modern humans originated in Africa because that's where they've found the oldest bones. Geneticists have come to the same conclusion by looking at Africa's vast genetic diversity, which could only have arisen as DNA mutated over millennia. There's less consensus about the routes our ancestors took in their journey out of Africa and around the planet. Early migrations stalled but left behind evidence such as a human skull from 92,000 years ago at Qafzeh, Israel. Those people may have taken a northern route through the Nile Valley into the Middle East. But other emigrants who left Africa tens of thousands of years later could also have taken a different route: across the southern end of the Red Sea. Scientists say these more recent wanderers gave rise to the 5.5 billion humans living outside Africa today.

1. African Cradle

   Most paleoanthropologists and geneticists agree that modern humans [Homo Sapiens] arose some 200,000 years ago in Africa. The earliest modern human fossils were found in Omo Kibish, Ethiopia. Sites in Israel hold the earliest evidence of modern humans outside Africa, but that group went no farther, dying out about 90,000 years ago.

2. Out of Africa

Genetic data show that a small group of modern humans left Africa for good 70,000 to 50,000 [Homo Sapiens] years ago and eventually replaced all earlier types of humans, such as Neandertals [Albion's/cavemen] and Homo Erectus. All non-Africans are the descendants of these travelers, who may have migrated around the top of the Red Sea or across its narrow southern opening[3].

Melanin in America

The first Americans were descended from Australian aborigines, according to evidence in a BBC documentary. The skulls suggest faces like those of Australian aborigines. The program, Ancient Voices, shows that ~~the dimensions of~~ prehistoric skulls found in Brazil match those of the aboriginal peoples of Australian and Melanesia. Other evidence suggest that these first Americans were later massacred by invaders from Asia.

Until now, native Americans were believed to have descended from Asian ancestors who arrived over a land bridge between Siberia and Alaska and then migrated across the whole of north and south America. The land bridge was formed 11,000 years ago during the ice age, when sea level dropped.

However, the new evidence shows that these people did not arrive in an empty wilderness. Stone tools and charcoal from the site in Brazil show evidence of human habitation as long ago as 50,000 years.

The skull dimensions and facial features match most closely the native people of Australia and Melanesia. These people date back to about 60,000 years, and were themselves descended from the first humans, who left Africa about 100,000 years ago.

Prevailing ideas point to all Native Americans descending from ancient Siberians who moved across the Beringialand bridge between Asia and North America between 26,000 and 18,000 years ago. As time wore on, the thinking goes, these people spread southward and gave rise to the Native American populations encountered by European settlers centuries ago.

But therein lies a puzzle: "Modern Native Americans closely resemble people of China, Korea, and Japan, but the oldest American skeletons do not," says archaeologist and paleontologist, lead author on the study and the owner of Applied Paleoscience, a research consulting service based in Bothell, Washington.

The small number of early American specimens discovered so far have smaller and shorter faces and longer and narrower skulls than later Native Americans, more closely resembling the modern people of Africa, Australia, and the South Pacific. "This has led to speculation that perhaps the first Americans and Native Americans ," Chatters continues, "or migrated from Asia at different stages in their evolution."[4]

Other evidence points to an early relationship between Africa and America. The discovery of American narcotics in Egyptian mummies has left some historians

---

[4] **Read more http://www.smithsonianmag.com/science-nature/dna-120 00-year-old-skeleton-helps-answer-question-who-were-first-americans -180951469/#SKTCtavR3JcX9x40.99.**

amazed. Recently, archaeologists discovered the presence of narcotics only known to be derived from American plants in ancient Egyptian mummies. These substances included South American cocaine from Erythroxylon and nicotine from Nicotiana tabacum. German toxicologist Svetla Balabanova reported the findings, which suggest that such compounds made their way to Africa through trans-Atlantic trade that would predate Columbus' arrival by thousands of years.

Melaninated Origins in China [Asia]

China is apparently finding out now what melaninated historians have been reporting for many years, the first inhabitants of China were in fact melaninated.

H. Imbert, a French anthropologist said in his book, "*Les Negritos de la Chine*","The Negroid races peopled at some time all the South of India, Indo-China and China. The South of Indo-China actually has now pure Negritos as the Semangs and mixed as the Malays and the Sakais."

Another author and professor, Chang Hsing-Lang, revealed similar information in writing "The Importation of Negro Slaves to China under the Tang Dynasty", "Even the sacred Manchu dynasty shows this Negro strain. The lower part of the face of the Emperor Pu-yi of Manchukuo, direct descendant of the Manchu rulers of China, is most distinctly Negroid."[5]

The Twa [Pygmies]

One of our oldest living ancestors are the Twa. The Twa are the origin of many concepts found in Kemet and Kush. The Hebrew creation story origins can be found in the Twa's story of the fall of humans which predate Hebrews by thousands of years.

The transition from hunting and gathering to farming involved a major cultural innovation that has spread rapidly over most of the globe in the last ten millennia. In sub-Saharan Africa, hunter-gatherers have begun to shift toward an agriculture-based lifestyle over the last 5,000 years. Only a few populations still base their mode of subsistence on hunting and gathering. The Twa are considered to be the largest group of mobile hunter-gatherers of Africa. They dwell in equatorial rainforests and are characterized by their short mean stature.

---

[5]DNA Evidence Proves That The First People In China Were Black by Daphne R

However, little is known about the chronology of the demographic events–size changes, population splits, and gene flow–ultimately giving rise to contemporary Pygmy (Western and Eastern) groups and neighboring agricultural populations. They have studied the branching history of Pygmy hunter-gatherers and agricultural populations from Africa and estimated separation times and gene flow between these populations. They resequenced 24 independent non coding regions across the genome, corresponding to a total of 33 kb per individual, in 236 samples from seven Pygmy and five agricultural populations dispersed over the African continent. They used simulation-based inference to identify the historical model best fitting our data. The model identified included the early divergence of the ancestors of Pygmy hunter-gatherers and farming populations 60,000 years ago, followed by a split of the Pygmies' ancestors into the Western and Eastern Pygmy groups 20,000 years ago. These findings increase knowledge of the history of the peopling of the African continent in a region lacking archaeological data. An appreciation of the demographic and adaptive history of African populations with different modes of subsistence should improve our understanding of the influence of human lifestyles on genome diversity.

Hallet, an author first shows that the Pygmies are certainly one of the oldest races on Earth. He then demonstrates that their legends and myths are likely the basis of much Egyptian myth, which in turn influenced biblical stories. Hence, there is no need to suppose that the Pygmies were influenced by Bible stories. In reality, there is absolutely no evidence of any such influence, including and especially in the Pygmy language, which would have reflected biblical intrusions such as the names of "Jesus" and "Moses," etc. In this regard, Hallet with his colleague Alex Pelle also created an 8,000-word Efé lexicon that reveals some stunning comparisons to various Indo-European languages, including and especially Germanic ones such as Old Norse/Norwegian. Again, it appears that this old and isolated people may be the originators of much language as well[6].

CHAPTER 3: RITES OF PASSAGE

United Nation # 215279514 * 1928 Cook County Registration # 1010590 5 on form 1099 book 521 page 579

Moorish Federal Consulate (901,251.1982) Diplomatic Consulate Post # 10105905-8321 Cook County Registry # 1122729006

Indigenous people across the earth incorporated rites of passage into their society. Melaninated indigenous people used rites of passage to cultivate society. According to *Africana Studies*, Five Major African Initiation Rites **Prof. Manu Ampim explains:**

There are five major African initiation rites which are fundamental to human growth and development. These rites were originally established by African ancestors while they were living in order to link the individual to the community and the community to the broader and more potent spiritual world. Initiation rites are a natural and necessary part of a community, as are arms and legs natural and necessary extension of the human body. These rites are critical to individual and community development, and it should not to be taken for granted that people automatically grow and develop into responsible, community-oriented adults.

The process of *initiation* concerns undergoing a fundamental set of rites to start a new phase or beginning in life. It marks the passing from one phase in life to the next more mature phase. *Initiation* fundamentally has to do with transformation, and has been a central component of traditional African cultures since time immemorial. The details of the rites vary among the different societies, but these rites are nevertheless basic components of the society as they help guide the person from one stage in life into the next stage of one's life and development, that is, from birth to death and beyond.

The five rites are **birth, adulthood, marriage, eldership, and *ancestorship*.** A rite is a fundamental act (or set of rituals) performed according to prescribed social rules and customs. Each of these rites are a key component that are a part of traditional African cultures. Some societies have more elaborate and extensive ceremonies than others, but these five themes are the thread that links families and villages in traditional Africa and provide the necessary structure for individual growth and development. The 5 rites briefly described below represent an integrated initiation system that has given indigenous African cultures the stability and longevity to provide a model of consistency and inter-generational unity. They represent a complete set of devices that prevent the inherent conflicts between various age groups or the systematic ill treatment of women, children, or elders. These problems are commonplace in western cultures, but they are virtually unknown in indigenous African cultures. These African cultures were not "perfect" as all human societies have problems, but they do provide a viable example in the modern world of how to solve social conflicts and contradictions and give individual the societal support to discover and fulfill their life mission and unique contribution.

Rite of Birth

The *Rite of Birth* is the first of the major African initiation rites and it involves initiating the infant into the world through a ritual and naming ceremony. Nearly all African indigenous cultures hold that the infant has come from the spirit world with important information from that world, and is bringing unique talents and gifts to offer to the community. The infant, in fact, is believed to have been commissioned to come to the world and accomplish a particular mission or project, and often has a great message to deliver.

Therefore, it is the responsibility of the family and community to discover the infant's unique mission through consultations with a diviner and to have rituals and a birth chart done. This is done to clearly determine the new community member's mission in order to guide him/her through their life path. The infant's name is given after the determination of the mission and it is a reflection of the infant's personality or the life mission itself.

Rite of Adulthood

The *Rite of Adulthood* is the second major initiation rite and it is nowadays the most popular among the set of rites. Most people today assume that "rites of passage" only refers to initiation into adulthood, and they are often not aware that adulthood rites are only one set of rites within a larger system of rites. Adulthood rites are usually done at the onset puberty age (around 12-13 years of age in many cultures) and they are to ensure the shaping of productive, community-oriented responsible adults. There is nothing automatic about youth being productive members of society, nor is there anything particularly difficult about transitioning from a child to an adult. This transition to adulthood is exceedingly difficult in Western societies because there are no systems of adulthood rites to systematically guide and direct the young person through this important stage in his or her life cycle.

In Western culture adulthood is seen as a status achieved at the age of 18 or 21, or simply when the person graduates from high school. Unfortunately, in most cases there is no fundamental guidance or transformation from a child to an adult that is required or expected. This "leave it for chance" approach to adulthood development is the root of most teenage and youth "adult" confusion, chaos, and uncertainty. When the youth reach a certain age, somehow they are expected to magically transformed into an "adult," eventhough they often receive very little guidance.

On the other hand, African societies systematically initiate boys and girls. They often take the young initiates out of the community, and away from the concerns of everyday life, to teach them all the ways of adulthood: including the rules and taboos of the society; moral instruction and social responsibility; and further clarification of his/her mission or calling in life.

Rite of Marriage

The *Rite of Marriage* is the third major initiation rite and it represents not only the joining of two families, but also the joining of the two missions of the new couple. In other words, the marriage rites are performed for not only the coming together of male and females to procreate and perpetuate life and the coming together of families, it is also an institution that helps both the husband and wife to best fulfill their mission and objectives in life. Unfortunately, in Western society a vast number of marriages fail as they are often based upon the couple "falling in love" and thereby entering the relationship in an unbalanced state. Individual often "fall in love" quick and "fall out of love" just as quickly, as soon as they recover from the emotional "love at first site" syndrome. African society, on the other hand, does not emphasize individual looks and lust as the primary motivation for marriage, but rather the basic focus is on building families and communities. The focus is on the collective more than the individual. A person is not generally considered an adult until they have married and had children.

Marriage is an important part of indigenous society. The union of two people to rear children is a major rite in the culture. Melaninated people across the globe adopted various practices of marriage. Multiple wives and families are very common among indigenous African culture. These concepts of marriage practice are called polygamy and polygny.

Polygny means: *the state or practice of having more than one wife or female mate at a time.*

Polygamy means: *marriage in which a spouse of either sex may have more than one mate at the same time.*

Native American Marriage Traditions

In addition, other Indigenous societies in America include another perspective into our widening understanding of self. This includes excerpts of an article on Native American's traditions on marriage.

Many white writers usually forget that "the American heritage" is a Native American heritage for 30 or 40,000 years! Certainly, the "common law" of First Americans should dominate any discussions but it is normally ignored.

Every tribe had its own specific traditions, but more importantly every mature individual was guided by his or her own dreams, visions, and personal spiritual calling.

Native communities usually were generally accepting of individual choices so long as they did not serve to damage others or the well-being of the whole. This meant that many tribes allowed couples wide latitude in the choice of how they decided to become bonded and with whom they would share their life (or lives).

Plural marriage was often common (usually one male, often older, with several women) as was the marriage of young men and women with older women and men, the age of their grandparents. In the latter case, the young partners would often marry someone younger or the same age after their older, first mate, had passed on.

Couples of the same sex also were recognized as legitimate in many or perhaps most tribes. This style of marriage may not have been overly common, but it is certainly noted for a number of American Nations.

As such, it forms part of the "common law" of North America and of the USA in particular.[7]

Scholars of the African traditional family agree that the one widely known aspect that distinguishes the African traditional family, from the European one, is the perversity of polygamy. Although polygamy is the act of an individual being married to more than one spouse at the same time, the more commonly practiced in Africa is polygyny "the legal marriage of one man to two or more women concurrently - is permitted." I argue that because of its perversity, the presence and absence of polygyny was a significant determinant and indicator of the nature of virtually every African social group; whether tribe, clan, or extended family, whether matrilineality or patrilineality was practiced, bride price existed, and how children were raised.

Polygyny was widely practiced in Africa and it often formed the backbone of the traditional African family patterns. According to Mair, "the polygynous joint family, consisting of a man, his wives, and their children, is the ideal for most Africans." Studies conducted from the 1930s to 1950s indicate that polygyny was common virtually in all regions of Africa.

In spite of the perversity of polygyny, there was evidence that it was on the decline. The major reason cited is that with increasing modern influences, marrying more than one wife became an economic burden. Even traditionally, ordinary citizens could not achieve marrying more than one wife. Often only Kings, chiefs and men who had wealth could afford it. Polygyny though set the tone and often determined the strength of the society and pattern of social organization of the traditional African family. The Baganda[8] people of Uganda provide the best illustration.

In the late and early 19th century, a detailed study

---

[8] Buganda is a subnation within Uganda [Wikipedia]

conducted among the Baganda found that, "Polygyny, the type of marriage in which the husband has plural wives, is not only the preferred but the dominant form of marriage for the Baganda." Commoners had two or three, chiefs had dozens, and the Kings had hundreds of wives. What was the structure of the polygynous family?

Although among the Baganda, the nuclear family of the mother, father, and their children constitutes the smallest unit of the Baganda kinship system, the traditional family consists of " several nuclear units held in association by a common father." Because the Baganda people are patrilineal, the household family also includes other relatives of the father such as younger unmarried or widowed sisters, aged parents, and children of the father's clan sent to be brought up by him. Included in this same bigger household will be servants, female slaves, and their children. The father remains the head of the nuclear family units.

Having so many people in this household should not be confused with other types of large families like, the 'joint' family, with its several married brothers and their families living together or the 'extended' family, consisting of a group of married off spring living in one household under a patriarch or matriarch." The Baganda are also patrilocal. Therefore, the new families tend to generally live near or with the husband's parents.

Rite of Eldership

The *Rite of Eldership* is the fourth major initiation rite and it is an important component of the initiation system, because it is the elders who represent tradition and the wisdom of the past. In African culture, there is a fundamental distinction that has to be made between an "elder" and "older" person. An older person has simply lived a longer life than most of people, but it not considered one who deserves high praise and respect. This is because the older person's life has not been a positive example for the community. An older person could be a thief or drunkard, an evil person, or could be someone who never married and had children, and thus these examples would certainly prevent a person from being considered a respected elder.

An elder, on the other hand, is someone who is given the highest status in African, indigenous culture because he or she has lived a life of purpose, and there is nothing more respected than living a purposeful life. The life of an elder is centered in the best tradition of the community, and is someone who has gone through all of the previous three rites, and is a living model for the other groups in the society to emulate. An elder is given the highest status and along with new infants because these two groups represent the closest links to the wisdom of the spirit world.

Rite of Ancestorship

The last of the five major rites is the *Rite of Ancestorship*, which concerns passing over into the spirit world. This final initiation rite is an extension of the elder/older distinction because the status that a person has in life is the *same status* that they bring with them when they pass on. There is virtually no African society that believes that when a person dies this ends all ties and communication with the living. Rather, African philosophy from one culture to another agrees that the spirit of the deceased is still with the living community, and that a distinction must be made in the status of the various spirits, as there are distinctions made in the status of the living.

One of the most important distinctions is the difference between an older person who dies and who is seen as nothing more than a "dead relative," and a respected elder who passes on and is revered as an honored "ancestor." The dead relative dies without honor and is someone who is not remembered as a great person or someone who should be followed or emulated. On the other hand, a respected elder who passes on becomes a respected ancestor and is given the highest honor. This group of ancestor wield great power and are often called upon in matters of trouble or uncertainty to help influence a favorable outcome. Thus, ancestors are respected elders who have passed away and who continue to serve as an extension of the family and community.

CHAPTER 4:
PRACTICAL APPLICATION

The above general outline of the African initiation rites is a summary of the complete system of rites that have enormous implications for Indigenous communities in various parts of the diaspora. These communities are struggling to find solid and lasting solutions to long standing problems, resulting from centuries of slavery and colonialism. The solution to these deep-rooted problems is to learn and apply the fundamental philosophies and principles that have created harmonious traditional African/Indigenous societies.

The five major initiation rites can be implemented in any Moorish, indigenous or any community that seeks to find solutions to the problem of a large number of people in the community who lack direction and purpose, and who lack a commitment to build and develop the community. The fact is that in order to produce a society that is focused on the best interest of the community requires a broad-based system that is designed to produce community-oriented responsible adults.

A few practical suggestions include the following:

Rite of Birth: a birth chart should be made for each infant or young person in each family. This is necessary in order to determine their personality, talents, and gifts. If this chart is done before the new baby is given a name, then the name will always remind the person of what their mission is in life whenever his/her name is called. When a person's name reflects their life's purpose then this is a powerful tool to help keep the person focused on their life's work.

Indigenous people should home birth, create indigenous birthing centers and use mid-wives instead of medical doctors, who are surgeons. The percentage rate of surgery by cesarean section is 32.7 percent[9]. Indigenous melaninated people do not file a Birth Certificate with a hospital or birthing center. It is necessary to file an Affidavit of Live Birth on a county level. The Affidavit of Live Birth is a legal remedy and alternative to state and Federal paperwork. The Affidavit of Live Birth is a contract between Mother, Father and child. This contract is very important in establishing status between the parents. Both parents are considered custodial and equal in status even if not legally married.

Indigenous people must avoid the State [statues] as much as possible. Established Moorish, indigenous people do not use State contracts for personal issues. This means the melaninated conscious person [male or female]

---

[9] **http://www.cdc.gov/nchs/fastats/delivery.html Center for Disease Co ntrol.**

does not use Child Support to create finance, as a remedy or retaliation against the other parent. Child Support is used only after all remedies for indigenous couple have been exhausted. After using an Affidavit of Live Birth, you should file it at the county level. In many counties, you can file it at the county recorder's office.

Avoiding the State[10] in family affairs is essential to a Free Person. The parents may need to create an Affidavit of Financial Responsibility. Parents may need to decide if they want this type of affidavit while together or after a possible break-up. This affidavit establishes both parental rights and obligations agreed between both parents. For example, it would express how much money father or mother would pay if separated or no longer in a relationship, days of visitation or shared parenting and penalties if either party [parent] default on contractual obligations. This creates a checks and balance system for parents. This keeps the mother from using Child Support as a weapon and the father from abandonment of his responsibilities.

Vaccinations should also be avoided. Each state is different however they will allow vaccination exemption.

---

[10] **The State is a jurisdiction used by government. It is also related to statuory law.**

An Affidavit of Exemption of Vaccination is recommended. Breast feeding is the natural way to build and create a baby's immunity.

Western societies are preoccupied with the sexual-esthetic function of the female breast. However, its true wonder lies in the power to lactate, the maternal attribute that has enabled mammals to survive over thousands of years. Breast-feeding practices have an important medical and socio-cultural role. Lactation has a direct beneficial effect on the infant in that it promotes its growth and normal development and confers protection against various infantile diseases, especially infections. In addition, lactation is far more than merely a biological fact: it is an aspect of "mothering", the culturally constructed bonding between a mother and her child.

A birthing center or centre is a healthcare facility, staffed by nurse-, and/or , for mothers in , who may be assisted by and coaches. By attending the laboring mother, the **doulas** can assist the midwives and make the birth easier. The midwives monitor the labor, and well-being of the mother and fetus during birth. Should additional medical assistance be required the mother can be transferred to a hospital. Some hospitals are now adding birth centers to their facilities as an alternative to the high tech maternity wards commonly found at most hospitals.

A birth center presents a more home-like environment than a, typically with more options during labor: food/drink, music, and the attendance of family and friends if desired. Other characteristics can also include non-institutional furniture such as queen-sized beds, large enough for both mother and father and perhaps birthing tubs or showers for. The decor is meant to emphasize the normality of birth. In a birth center, women are free to act more spontaneously during their birth, such as squatting, walking or performing other postures that assist in labor. Active birth is encouraged. The length of stay after a birth is shorter at a birth center; sometimes just 6 hours after birth the mother and infant can go home[11].

A doula (/ˈduːlə/), also known as a birth companion and post-birth supporter,[1] is a nonmedical person who assists a woman before, during, and/or after childbirth, as well as her spouse and/or family, by providing physical assistance and emotional support. The provision of continuous support during labour is associated with improved maternal and fetal health and a variety of other

---

[11] **Wikipedia. http://en.wikipedia.org/wiki/Birthing_center**

benefits, including lower risk of induction and interventions and less need for pain relief. These benefits are particularly significant when continuous support is provided by someone who is not there as family/friend or as medical staff (i.e. a doula). Additionally, a doula is sometimes hired to work with families beyond the postpartum stages, providing continued physical and emotional support, for as long as needed (sometimes, this support can be ongoing for several years)[12].

Rite of Adulthood: the adulthood rites have to be seen in a larger context. Most programs are well meaning but the problem is often that the mentors of the numerous adulthood "rites of passage" programs have not been initiated themselves. It is obvious that one cannot teach what one has not been taught. The African proverb is that "one who learns, teaches." The solution to this contradiction is for there to be more focus on programs or organizations for men and women to deal with their own issues of a lack of self-development and lack of a purposeful life, so that they could be better examples for the youth. In other words, the principles that are taught must be applied to the lives of the mentors and adults,

---

[12]**AFRICANA STUDIES Five Major African Initiation Rites Prof. Manu A mpim.**

otherwise the programs have no credibility or long term effectiveness.

Rite of Marriage: the solution to the epidemic of serial marriages – where many individual marry and divorce multiples times during the course of their life is to change the approach from off-balanced individuals "falling in love" to the more balanced and stable approach of culturally-centered families forming a mutual bond. The problem for many so called Black people is that they often adopt anti-social Western ideas and thus see in-laws as their opponents. If more marriages were formed between individuals that have both been through the birth and adulthood rites, then more unions would work because both individuals would have a clear focus in life and would also know how to best support the other partner's mission. They would be marrying the person *and* their mission.

Indigenous society must reintroduce multiple spouses into indigenous society. Polygny is an intricate part of our past and is seen today in perverted ways i.e. pimps, players and ballers. The idea of a Western monogamous relationship is incomplete and not working in the present melaninated community. The average melaninated male fails to marry because of the limitations modern Western marriages provide. Men become dis-honest with their spouse because fear of her finding "out". The "baby mama" syndrome is very common and accepted in the "Black" community. Young melaninated people today have casual sex, children out of wedlock and child support problems [financial problems]. Westernized ideology places melaninated people into the State's jurisdiction. Polygny would create an environment where there would be multiple incomes, homeschooling environment, large families, whole family structure and financial security.

The remedy to avoiding a Marriage license is to use an Affidavit of Common Law Marriage. Affidavit's work in place of a License, taking you outside State's jurisdiction. An Affidavit, like a Marriage License, is a contract. Indigenous free people have the right to contract as consenting adults. Contracts can be enforced through court if needed. Contracts can be tailored to fit the requirements of the couple. In the case of polygny or any other form of marriage.

Rite of Eldership: every Moorish, indigenous, African centered community should establish a *council of* *elders* to help guide that particular community. There are a number of examples of African societies govern by elders (gerontocracy) because of their collective and accumulative wisdom. This is an important philosophy that should be adopted because a *council of elders* could be consulted in a variety of matters, ranging from family or marriage disputes, community-wide issues, naming of buildings and community centers, and directing resources to supporting important projects. The guidelines of choosing the council members should be clearly established and members chosen by vote. Without a *council of elders* most Black communities will remain disorganized and lacking direction and effective leadership.

A council of elders were created in Dayton [New Kemit], Ohio's African and Moorish centered community. The council's goal is to give guidance to the community. The Council of Elders is to develop and increase appreciation for elders and youth and their contributions to community development.

Believing that education is the intergenerational transmission of the wisdom of the ancestors, which begins with the original message from the Creator to speak truth and to do justice, The Council of Elders is a circle of men and women elders of African American or other African lineage. The Council of Elders is rooted in the seven principles of Kwanzaa- to advance the collective well being of African Americans and other peoples of African lineage in Dayton, Ohio. Dayton Africana Council of Elders: Frankie Earl, Bakari Lumumba, Jesse O. Gooding, Margaret Evelyn Peters, Ahminullah Ahmad, Willis Bing Davis, Floyd B. Johnson, Tony Brooks, Robert E. Jones, Nozipo Glenn, Don Black, William B. Schooler, Greer Stanford-Randle, Claude (Yaya) Fambrough, David K. Greer, Dr. Boikai Twe, Viennease Dennis, Annette McGee Wright, Clay Dixon, Robert Walker, Mwesi Chu (John Taylor), Dr. Morris Brown, Vernellia R. Randall[13].

Rite of Ancestor ship: every Moorish community that establishes a governing council of elders should also chose a group of local and national ancestors whose life represented a purpose focused on helping (in some way) to build and develop the community. This local group of honorable ancestors should be chosen to be remembered because of their great example and contributions, and thus their life should be honored. Too often when ancestors are remembered during community ceremonies a

---

[13]African American Cultural fest Dayton, Ohio.

distinction is not made between respected ancestors and dead relatives, or another problem is that many times *famous* ancestors are remembered but *local* ancestors are overlooked during these ceremonies. Every healthy community must have *local* (s)heros[14].

One major acknowledgement of our ancestors is the process of libation. Pour libation for your father and mother who rest in the valley of the dead. God will witness your action and accept it. Do not forget to do this even when you are away from home. For as you do for your parents, your children will do for you also. This ancient proverb is a classic outlook of indigenous libations. Libation connects the living with the deceased. Here is an example of libation.

On the matter of what to offer the Ancestor or Deities, we have the choice of Water, Wine and "Hard" Liquor. The choice of liquid depends on the nature of the libation and prayer and what your aim is in invoking (awakening) the Ancestors.

As has been my own experience:

Water is for cooling and healing and creating or reconciling relationships.

[14] **Africana Studies, Five Major African Initiation Rites Professor Manu Ampi m**

Liquor is fiery and is usually used to rouse, cement, ignite, protect and peform strong purfication.

Wine is mid-way between the two and is good for friendly relations, creating comradery between man and spirit.

This is an important matter as many of us do not realize that when you pour libation you are awakening the Ancestors. The libation is only the 1st part of the process. After awakening the Ancestors, we have to actually do something, discuss something or work a ritual. Libation is not complete without at bare minimum thanking the Ancestors or requesting something like support, stability, clarity, spiritual cleansing or protection and etc[15].

Ancestral Money

If there is indeed such a thing as afterlife, the Chinese and Vietnamese might just be the richest people there. And that's because their living relatives make sure they are well provided for by throwing money into flames. Well, not real money. Only fake

---

[15] **Libation: Africa Speaks.com**

notes. This fake money is commonly known as ghost money, "Joss paper" and as 'pinyin' (literally 'shade' or 'dark' money) in Chinese. The ghost money, along with other papier-mâché items (usually expensive stuff) are burned as a part of Chinese tradition – on holidays to venerate the deceased, and also at funerals, to make sure that the spirits have plenty of good things in the afterlife.

Traditionally, Joss paper is made from coarse bamboo paper or rice paper. The Joss is cut into squares or rectangles and has a thin piece of square foil glued in the center. Sometimes, it is even endorsed with a traditional Chinese red ink seal depending on the particular region. The paper is generally of a white color (symbolizing mourning) and the foil is either silver or gold (representing wealth), hence the name, ghost money. The three types of ghost money are copper (for newly deceased spirits and spirits of the unknown), gold (for the deceased and the higher gods), and silver (for ancestral spirits and local deities). Sometimes Joss paper is completely gold, engraved with towers or ingots. The burning of joss paper is not done casually, but with a certain reverence, placed respectfully in a loose bundle. Some other customs involve folding each sheet in a specific manner before burning. The burning is mostly done in an earthenware pot or a chimney built specifically for this purpose.

Contemporary forms of joss money are rather different; they look more like the money from current times. Westernized varieties include copies of Bank notes (Chinese Yuan, Thai Baht, Vietnamese Dong, or even the US Dollar), cheques and paper credit cards. Some people even go as far as offering papier-mâché houses, cars, toilets, servants, passports, flight tickets, rice cookers and even flat-screen TVs. Any object that can carry a brand will be branded with the most extravagant options. No luxuries are denied to the deceased. The bank notes are specifically meant for dead ancestors to give as a tribute to the God of Death for a short stay or to escape punishment. The bank note copies are often of outrageous denomination they can range anywhere between $10,000 and $5,000,000,000. These notes carry an image of the 'Bank of Hell' on the back and the Jade Emperor on the front.

The practice of burning spirit or ghost money is quite deep-rooted in Asian culture. According to

archeological evidence, the tradition can be traced back to 1000 BC. Even back then, imitations of what could only be considered money were left within tombs. Clay imitations of gold plaques were found, along with stone imitations of lead and bronze money. The Chinese believe that all those who die, automatically gain entry into the underworld of Diyu. They are judged there, before being sent to heaven, the underworld, or for reincarnation. 'Hell' in itself is not viewed as a place of torture, but a more neutral realm. The paper money is believed to be deposited in an afterlife bank of sorts, from which the deceased spirits can make withdrawals. The ritual is said to be derived from a mix of regional folklore and Taoism. The practice of ancestor worship is largely religious, stemming from the fact that the spirits of the deceased are still interested in the affairs of the world. Keeping them happy brings blessings from them for the living. Another explanation for the concept is that the living are allowed to ask spirits to fulfill their wishes, for which they are indebted. This debt cannot be entirely cleared off while alive, so the ghost money sent after death is used to repay whatever they owe the spirits. Buddhists, however, discourage the practice of burning joss paper, saying that the deceased would have no interest over worldly items, and that it is also not too great for the environment[16].

Ancestor Ascension

The Ancestor Ascension Ceremony is not a memorial ceremony to note or mourn the loss of loved one but to acknowledge and elevate our ancestors as 'worthy of living forever'. Additionally, this is a healing ceremony to recognize our family members and friends who have become ancestors and are worthy of acknowledgement and living forever. This should be practiced in all communities.

CHAPTER 5:

EUROCENTRICITY AND THE TRADITIONAL AFRICAN FAMILY

Patrilineality, matrilineality, and the practice of polygyny are three of the major distinguishing

[16] **Ghost Money - Currency of the Afterlife, by Sumitra**

variations of the African traditional extended family. The literature on the subject is truly as vast and reflects traditional patterns that are as diverse as the variations of the physical looks of the people found on the continent. What is significant about the various descriptions of the traditional African family is that they are from back in the period before the 1940s and in case of the Baganda from the late 1800s. Social change in Africa as everywhere else is ubiquitous. Such influences as end of intra and inter-tribal warfare with the coming of European colonialism, the Western money economy, industrialization, migration, and urbanization have certainly transformed the traditional African family from what it was 50 to 100 years ago. By 1935, for example, anthropologists like Mair and Richards and no doubt many others were already noticing change in marriage and family patterns[17].

The written descriptions and therefore perceptions of the traditional African family were also a victim of the European colonial cultural bias and Christian

---

[17] p. 37 Lucy P.Mair "African Marriage and Social Change," in Survey of Afri can Marriage and Family life, Edited by Arthur Phillips, (London: Oxford Un iversity Press, 1953) p. 51 Naboth M. J. Ngulube, Some Aspects of Growing U p in Zambia, (Lusaka: Nalinga Consultacy/Sol-Consult A/S Limited, 1989)

values. In a more obvious way, this Euro-centrism[18] did not treat polygamy, the African marriages and the extended family and any others of its "eccentricities" (regarded as such because they were different from European customs) as social phenomena that was legitimate and workable in its own African social circumstances and environment. But rather as curiosities that were to succumb to the superior European monogamous marriage values legitimated by Christianity.

Some of the issues that were the products of the Euro-centrically biased judgments include the following two. First, the strengths, durability, and resilience of the African traditional family were never dwelt on explicitly and at length. For example, in the polygynous African family, like among the Baganda, and many others, your father's wives and brothers were not just mothers and fathers just as mere kinship terms. These carried with them all the heavy social obligations demanded of a mother or father, daughter or son. There was never a distinction between the biological and non-biological kin as far as primary parental obligations were concerned.

[18] **TRADITIONAL MARRIAGES IN ZAMBIA A Studyin Cultural History Y izenge A. Chondoka M.A. 1988**

Other significant strengths are that the traditional African family increased group cohesion in an otherwise harsh physical and social environment.

Second, the continued Euro-centric descriptions and characterization of the African traditional family as somewhat depraved lead to the use of such terms as bride price, avoidance social taboos, segregated relationships, lack of "love" and "tenderness" in African marriages and families.

The continued, persistent and wide use of the term "bride price" to describe the valuables that were often given to the bride's parents before marriage was legitimated is one excellent example of evaluating and perceiving a custom from a biased Eurocentric perspective. Indeed, such authors as Chondoka[19] have recently found little accuracy or justification in calling this custom "purchasing" or "buying" of a wife. In fact Chondoka finds the use of the terms "dowry", "bride price" to refer to particularly traditional Zambian marriages to be serious misnomers introduced by European missionaries and colonialists in Africa. "There

---

[19]Lucy P. Mair, "**African Marriage and Social Change,**" p. 126

is no bride price in our society. Traditionally no parent fixes a price for his daughter (a bride). If he did, it would be like selling her. We do not sell brides in our society. However, as a prospective husband, you are told to pay for the marriage and not the bride. Marriage involves much more than just the bride."

People would further argue that among the African people that are conductors, participants, and are actors in these marriages, the concept "buy", "purchase" a wife or bride does not exist. For example, among the Tumbuka[20] of Eastern Zambia the verb kugula (to buy) is used to refer to purchasing of material objects or commodities and domestic animals. The verb kulobola is very specific meaning the valuables that are given partially or in full to the girl's people to legitimate or seal the marriage. Lobola is widely used among the Bantu peoples of Central and Southern Africa[21].

"Avoidance", "segregated relationships", lack of "love" and "tenderness" in traditional African marriages and the family has been a common theme among European scholars. These views were expressed before 1930s and as

---

[20] Ibid., p.131

[21] **Ibid., p. 131**

late as 1960s. LeVine[22] described some of the customs and patterns that surround interaction in the traditional African family as "institutionalized restrictions", "segregated patterns", and "avoidance patterns". These relationships which are described in this way are rituals of respect between a son-in-law and his mother-in-law, a daughter-in-law and her father-in-law. Similar customs or "rules of restrictions" in interaction apply between many other kin in a traditional African family. These Anglo-Saxon or Eurocentric descriptions do not help in the fair and accurate perception of the traditional African family. "The descriptions implicitly portray (to the African and Westerner) African relationships as being negative, rigid and miserable. Anything described in these terms must inherently be bad, primitive and, therefore, undesirable."[23]

Typical of this Eurocentric characterization of the traditional African family is often not only the contention that there cannot be genuine love in a polygamous marriages but that even monogamous ones lack "genuine" love. Some have even gone as far as saying that for the

---

[22] **Molefi Kete Asante, Afrocentricity: The Theory of Social Change. (B uffalo: Amulefi Publishing Company, 1980).**

[23] **Yizenge A. Chondoka, Tradional Marriage in Zambia: A Study in Cult ural History. (Ndola: Mission Press, 1988)**

African husband nothing else matters so long as he impregnates his wife every few years.[24] In the study of the Baganda traditional family cited earlier, the author describes how children are raised among the Baganda. The author describes the interaction between the Baganda mother and her baby as unfavorable and lacking any affection or love. "The mother may hug or caress the child and comfort it when hurt or in distress. However, children are never kissed because kissing is not known to the Baganda and the close intimacy of the mother child relationship as found in America, for example, is not present. The language of the Baganda carries no word for love or tender affection; the closest is a word that is best translated as "like"[25].

The issue to emphasize, is not so much that there are no weaknesses or shortcomings in the traditional African family, but that the Eurocentric Anglo-Saxon descriptions (that are believed to be objective and describe social phenomena as accurately as possible) eliminate, and over shadow the strengths and positive aspects that might have existed and may still exist in the African traditional family patterns.

[24] Ibid., p. 15

[25] Lucy P Mair "African Marriage and Social Change p. 14

The common descriptions of the African traditional family in the literature is Eurocentric and biased. Caution should be applied when sweeping generalizations are made which make the traditional African family is made to appear static, rigid, and lacking in vitality.

Indigenous Americans View of Love

Traditional Native American legends about love are sometimes a little curious to a modern American audience, because unlike classical mythology and European folktales, the Native American love stories rarely directly mention love. In fact, it is usually only in trickster tales and other funny stories that Native American characters announce "I love you" to each other. In most Native American oral traditions, it isn't typical for a storyteller to have serious characters talk or think aloud about how they are feeling a character's emotions are usually shown through actions, not by monologues. So just as Native American storytellers are more likely to describe a character crying than feeling sad or saying "I am sad," characters are also more likely to show their love through actions-- either positive actions such as sacrificing for the other person, going to great lengths to be together, or forgiving each other after a transgression, or sometimes negative actions such as jealous attacks or obsessive behavior. In classic American Indian love stories, the word "love" may never even be mentioned, but both the man and the woman will be observed to take at least one direct action to choose the other. Of course, modern Native American storytellers telling stories in English will sometimes choose to converse with the audience more than they might have in their native languages, so you sometimes will indeed hear Native American authors describing their heroes and heroines falling in love. But if you're reading older texts and you wonder why they seem so unromantic, try listening for the things the characters do for each other, not what they have to say.

CHAPTER 6: POLYGAMY THE NEW MONOGAMY

The Three Reasons for Polygamy[26]

Polygamy: a bird's eye view

There are three basic reasons for polygyny in birds. First, there may be a scarcity of adult males. Second,

[26] **Why the Obamas and the Romney's had Multiple Wives, Published on October 23, 2012 by Nigel Barber PHD, in The Human Beast.**

some males may have much better genes than others which is particularly important for populations where there is a heavy load of diseases and parasites to which resistance is genetically heritable. Third, females do better by sharing a mate who defends a good territory (with plenty of food and cover) than they would by opting to be the single mate in a bad territory.

Why the developed [Westernized] world hates polygamy?

At least three factors are critical. First, instead of a scarcity of males, developed countries have an excess thanks to better public health that saves more males than females.   Second, colder winters made it impossible historically for mothers to raise children without substantial help from their husbands.

The most important reason that polygamy is out of place in the modern world is that it works best in agricultural societies where children contribute to farm labor and care of livestock.

Developed countries are highly urbanized and it is very difficult to raise large families in cities because children are a huge drain on finances that lasts for two decades thanks to the extent of modern education. In agricultural societies, by contrast, children defray the expense of raising them by contributing productive labor to the household economy.

However, according to Census 2000, 281.4 million people were counted in the United States - 143.4 million of whom were female and 138.1 million male. About a 1434/1381 ratio women/men. In the United States woman outnumber men by 5 million. The ability for every woman to marry or to have a companion may not be possible. This also refutes the previous paragraph of thought.

Christianity and Polygamy

The modern world is structured around western and Christians values. Indigenous melaninated people suffer greatly under other religious cultures. Polygamy is considered sinful and against Christian doctrine. However, upon further review, the New Testament never speaks against polygny. Due to Catholic and Protestant dominant idealogy, many Christians are misled about marriage and polygamy.

There is not a single verse from the New Testament prohibits polygamy. Christians usually mistakenly present the following verses from the Bible to prove that polygamy in the New Testament is not allowed:

Matthew 19:1-12 "1. When Jesus had finished saying these things, he left Galilee and went into the region of Judea to the other side of the Jordan.
2. Large crowds followed him, and he healed them there.
3. Some Pharisees came to him to test him. They asked, "Is it lawful for a man to divorce his wife for any and every reason?"
4. "Haven't you read," he (Jesus) replied, "that at the beginning the Creator `made them male and female,'
5. and said, `For this reason a man will leave his father and mother and be united to his wife, and the two will become one flesh' ?
6. So they are no longer two, but one. Therefore what God has joined together, let man not separate."
7. "Why then," they asked, "did Moses command that a man give his wife a certificate of divorce and send her away?"
8. Jesus replied, "Moses permitted you to divorce your

wives because your hearts were hard. But it was not this way from the beginning.
9. I tell you that anyone who divorces his wife, except for marital unfaithfulness, and marries another woman commits adultery."
10. The disciples said to him, "If this is the situation between a husband and wife, it is better not to marry."
11. Jesus replied, "Not everyone can accept this word, but only those to whom it has been given.
12. For some are eunuchs because they were born that way; others were made that way by men; and others have renounced marriage because of the kingdom of heaven. The one who can accept this should accept it."

Also, *when a man becomes a one flesh with his wife in Matthew 19:5-6, this doesn't mean that the man can't be one flesh with another woman. He can be one flesh with his first wife, and one flesh with his second wife, and one flesh with his third wife and so on....*

To further make the point, look at the following from the New Testament:

Matthew 22:23-32 *"23. That same day the Sadducees, who say there is no resurrection, came to him with a question.*
24. "Teacher," they said, "Moses told us that if a man dies without having children, his brother must marry the

widow and have children for him.
25. Now there were seven brothers among us. The first one married and died, and since he had no children, he left his wife to his brother.
26. The same thing happened to the second and third brother, right on down to the seventh.
27. Finally, the woman died.
28. Now then, at the resurrection, whose wife will she be of the seven, since all of them were married to her?"
29. Jesus replied, "You are in error because you do not know the Scriptures or the power of God.
30. At the resurrection people will neither marry nor be given in marriage; they will be like the angels in heaven.
31. But about the resurrection of the dead--have you not read what God said to you,
32. `I am the God of Abraham, the God of Isaac, and the God of Jacob' ? He is not the God of the dead but of the living."

In Matthew 22:24-28, the Jews referred to Deuteronomy 25:5 from the Old Testament where it states that if a woman's husband dies, and she didn't have any kids from him, then she must marry his brother regardless whether he had a wife or not. When the Jews brought this situation up to Jesus in Matthew 22:24-28, Jesus did not prohibit at all for the childless widow to marry her husband's brother (even if he were married). Instead, Jesus replied to them by saying that we do not marry in heaven, and we will be like angels in heaven (Matthew 22:30).

So in other words, if Jesus [Yashua] allowed for a widow to marry her former husband's brother even if he were married, then this negates the Christians' claim about the Bible prohibiting polygamy. A man can be one flesh with more than one woman. In the case of Matthew 22:24-28, the man can be one flesh with his wife, and one flesh with his deceased brother's wife. Also keep in mind that Exodus 21:10 allows a man to marry an infinite amount of women, and Deuteronomy 21:15 allows a man to marry more than one wife.

Deuteronomy 21:15 *"When a man has two wives, one loved and the other unloved, and they have borne him children, both the loved and the unloved, and the first-born son is of her who is unloved".*

Many Biblical characters had multiple wives. Abraham had three wives [Sarah, Katurah and Hagar], Solomon is said to had three hundred wives and seven hundred concubines. An article by Naftali Silberberg states:

The Torah does not forbid a man from having multiple wives. Abraham, Jacob, David and Solomon are notable examples of biblical figures who wedded more than one wife.

A close reading, however, reveals that in virtually all cases where our forefathers took multiple wives, it was for a specific reason. Abraham married Hagar only after Sarah suggested that he do so because she and Abraham had no children together. Another classic example is Jacob. He married Leah only because he was tricked into it by Laban. Similarly, he took Bilhah and Zilpah at the advice of his first two wives, who wished to bear children through them.

Yet the Torah does not outlaw polygamy.

Approximately one thousand years ago, the noted German scholar Rabbi Gershom "the Light of the Diaspora" banned polygamy. This ban was accepted as law by all Ashkenazic Jews, but was not recognized by Sephardic and Yemenite communities[27].

---

[27] **Does Jewish Law Forbid Polygamy? By Naftali Siberberg**

CHAPTER 7:

INDIGENOUS SPIRITUALITY

Spirituality is in the eye of the believer and with our ancient creeds, we find religion of our ancestors become important in regaining indigenous self. Spirituality of indigenous people reflects their relationship with earth and community. Among the spiritual practices of indigenous people, Vodoo is a perfect example of indigenous spiritual life.

Animism is a religious belief that sees non-human entities having a certain principle about life, that makes them spiritual beings. Animism is generally believed by native people following ancient folklore in Africa, South America, Australia and Southern Asia. Animism believes that not only humans but all natural phenomena, natural objects, and the universe, embody a soul or spirit. Animists propagate the doctrine that the soul is the main driving force of life and health. Animists revere the various spirits of nature such as the spirit of rain, wind, animals, forest, and earth and believe in maintaining harmony with the powers of nature.

Vodun, also known as Vudun or Voodoo, dating back 6,000 years, is a religion of coastal West Africa, stretching from Nigeria to Ghana. Vodun is practiced by some of the peoples in the following areas: Ghana, Togo, Benin, and Nigeria.

West African Vodun is the original form of the religions of Voodoo and Vodou found in the Americas including Haiti, the Caribbeans, and southern United States.

Vodun beliefs are built around spirits and other elements of divine origin which govern the human world. The hierarchy of these beings ranges from major gods governing the elements, as well as human society, to vodun that deal with more minor concerns such as streams, trees, rocks, certain clans and tribes, or nations.

Believers of Vodun emphasize ancestor worship and believe that humans and spirits occupy the same plane of existance. Each family of spirits is believed to have its own female priest, which is usually passed on from mother to daughter. Vodun religions include Yoruba, and Santeria Close to 30 million people in Africa practice West African Vodun.

The Loa are the children of Lusa (Lisa) and Mawu, members of an extra-dimensional race of beings known as the Orishas who were worshipped as gods by the natives of ancient Africa. The Orishas were the deities of the myriad Afrikaan tribes of Africa, but by in the 17th Century, Europeans invading the continent began abducting and taking whole tribes to use as servile servants or slaves in Europe and the Americas. Many slaves were removed from the Yoruba, Fon, Ewe, Dahomey tribes of Africa to use as slaves. Several Africans were treated respectively, but countless more were reduced to servile positions with little or no regard to their human conditions. The Africans called out to their ancient deities for solace, even combining tenets of

Catholicism and the Holy Roman Church into their rites, and the god Legba rallied his brothers and sisters into granting hope and promise to their suffering worshippers as the Loa. Worship of the Loa eventually became the religion of Voodoo through the descendants of the Africans removed from their homeland although the Gods Damballah and Sagbata introduced some sinister and malevolent aspects to the religion. Today, Voodoo and its rival practice of Santeria is practiced in most of the Caribbean and along the Gulf of Mexico down into South America. Most worshippers of Voodoo are African in origin, although some people of European descent have tapped into the darker arts of the religion for materialistic gains.

The Loa possess the conventional physical attributes of the African gods. Like all of the African gods, they are exceptionally long-lived, but they are not immortal: they tend to age extremely slowly since reaching adulthood and cannot die by any conventional means. They are immune to all Earthly diseases and are resistant to conventional injury. If somehow wounded, a Loa's godly life force would enable them to recover with superhuman speed. It would take an injury of such magnitude that it dispersed a major portion of their bodily molecules to cause a physical death. Even then, it might be possible for a god of significant power, such as <u>Nyambe</u> or for a number of African gods of equal power working together to revive him. Each of the Loa also possesses some measure of superhuman strength and their Orishas metabolism provide them with far greater than human endurance in all physical activities. (Orishas flesh and bone is about three times as dense as similar human tissue, contributing to the superhuman strength and weight of the African gods.)

Several members of the Loa have the ability to tap into and manipulate mystical energies, usually somewhere along the lines of their position or expertise, i.e. Damballah can tap into the power of the underworld while Shango can manipulate the forces of the weather. The majority of the Loa have certain powers in common such as traveling between dimensions, such as from Ala to Earth, and altering their appearance.

Indigenous American Spirituality

The relationship between America [Al-Moroc], Africa, Asia and Australia is ancient. Knowledge of self spread through the world in myth, astrology and sacred geometry.

Each time a creator-god would take a turn being the sun. Finally the gods had a council, and decided one of them would have to sacrifice himself to be the new sun. Nanauatl, a lowly, humble god became the sun, but there was a problem he wasn't moving. The gods realized that they all must sacrifice themselves so that humans could live. The god Ehecatl[28] sacrificed the others, and a mighty wind arose to move the sun at last.

This was no free sacrifice, however. Not only would the people have to help this weak sun to keep moving, they would also be responsible to repay the sacrifice. The world remained in a precarious position.

Once the sun was dealt with, the world had to be recreated. Quetzalcoatl (meaning *feathered serpent*) was the one who would create humans. Of course, people had been created several times before, so Quetzalcoatl descended into the underworld to retrieve their bones. He tripped as he fled, and the bones shattered into different

---

[28] **Ehecatl is a pre-Columbian deity associated with wind interperted as the aspect of Quetzacoatl.**

sized pieces, which is why people are all different sizes. By adding his own blood to the mix, people came to life.

The Calendar and the Sun

The ancient Aztec religion was highly focused on keeping nature in balance. One false step could lead to natural disaster. The weak sun could stop moving. In the sky was a constant battle between light and darkness, a battle that would someday be lost.

Huitzilopochtli (*Hummingbird of the South*) was the warrior sun (either the sun god or the one who fights for the sun god, Tonatiuh (the name given to Nanauatl)). Huitzilopochtli (or Tonatiuh) needed blood sacrifice in order to win the battle against darkness. Either there would be ritual blood-letting, or actual people would be sacrificed. Those sacrificed would rise to fight with him. And so human sacrifices became more and more common in Mexico. Often battles would be fought just to capture prisoners to sacrifice the Aztec flower war (or Aztec flowery war).

Every 52 years, the people were terrified that the world would end. All religious fires were extinguished, people all over the empire would destroy their furniture and precious belongings and go into mourning. When the constellation of the Pleiades appeared, the people would be assured that they were safe for another 52 years[29].

Creating an Altar

Indigenous people are known to create alters to give homage to their ancestors and deities. It is way to communicate with the spiritual world. Spiritualist maintain a connection with the supernatural and universe through the powerful use of the altars.

An ancestor altar is an effective and beautiful way to connect with and gain support from the spirit world. It can be as simple as a photograph and a glass of water, or as elaborate as the spirits direct.

A simple but well-made food offering to an adopted ancestor.

---

[29] http://www.aztec-history.com/ancient-aztec-religion.html

An even stronger connection than a photograph is a little dirt from your ancestors' graves. There is an art to getting that dirt in a respectful manner.

Go to the grave, bringing with you a small container such as a pill bottle, a spoon or trowel, a few coins and (if your ancestor has no history of alcoholism), a small bottle of whiskey. Introduce yourself to your ancestor. Explain what you want to do — bring home a little dirt from the grave so that you can build a connection with him or her. Pour the whiskey over the grave and tuck the coins into the grass about where your ancestor's hand would be. Then spoon a small quantity of dirt into the pill bottle.

When you get home, put the graveyard dirt into an attractive, appropriately sized container. Definitely something nicer than a pill bottle or zip lock bag. I have dirt from several graves; some of them, are kept in the sort of gold and silver-papered cardboard boxes that jewelers sometimes pack rings and earrings in.

A spiritual altar is, at its simplest, a focal point for self-reflection and contemplation on the divine. It can be highly religious in a formal sense or more spontaneous and intuitive. A spiritual altar is your personal space, so it should represent you and your understanding. Placing items on the altar is a meditational act in itself, as it reflects on the item's meaning and even ritualize its placement. Sometimes you reference a text to get further understanding of the concept associated with the chosen item. Altars, or shrines as they are called are very personal and will grow with you as your understanding grows.

Moorish Connection

The creed of our ancient ancestors are older than Hebrew, Christianity and Islam. Noble Drew Ali taught that Moor's were ancient Moabites. He also taught that Ham and Canaan divided Africa among themselves[30]. Islamism is called that Old time religion. Islamism is a term that denotes something similar but not the same as Islam. The term Islamism, as discussed in my other books, completely represents Gnostic teachings. Islamism is used to describe an ancient spiritual system found throughout the world. Old time religion as Islamism is describing the indigenous spiritual practices of Canaan, Kemet, Kush, Nubia, Libya and Sumer. The

---

[30] **Circle Seven Koran**

74

Tree of Life is the basis of many ancient spiritual systems all over the world. The Tree of Life and Islamism [old time religion] attempts to reconnect humans to their culture and higher self.

The Tree of Life in its various forms are recognized in all cultures as a symbol of immortality and eternal life. From ancient Chinese and Egyptian culture to Germanic paganism and Mesoamerica, it has been sought after throughout the ages. And, while depicted in many different contexts, the imagery across all cultures is essentially the same. Not to be confused with the Tree of Knowledge of Good and Evil, the tree of Life is the tree whose fruit gives eternal life to all who might obtain it. In addition to its religious references, it is a reminder of our past (roots - ancestry), present (tree body - knots included) and future (fruit – labor and posterity).

In Egyptian mythology, Auset and Ausar are the first couple, said to have emerged from the acacia tree of Saosis, which the Kemetians considered the Tree of Life. The Egyptians Holy Sycamore also stood on the threshold of life and death, connecting the two worlds.

In the system of , the first couple, apart from and (moisture and dryness) and and (earth and sky), are and . They were said to have emerged from the tree of , which the Egyptians considered the tree of life, referring to it as the "tree in which life and death are enclosed." Acacia trees contain DMT, a psychedelic drug associated with spiritual experiences. A much later myth relates how Set(h) killed Ausar, putting him in a coffin, and throwing it into the , the coffin becoming embedded in the base of a tamarisk tree[31].

The religion of the Canaanites was an agricultural religion, with pronounced fertility motifs. Their main gods were called the Baalim (Lords), and their consorts the Baalot (Ladies), or Asherah (singular), usually known by the personal plural name Ashtoret. The god of the city of Shechem, which city the Israelites had absorbed peacefully under Joshua, was called Baal-berith (Lord of the Covenant) or El-berith (God of the Covenant). Shechem became the first cultic center of the religious tribal confederacy (called an amphictyony by the Greeks) of the Israelites during the period of the judges. When Shechem was excavated in the early 1960s, the temple of Baal-berith was partially reconstructed; the sacred pillar (generally a phallic symbol or, often, a representation of the Ashera, the female fertility symbol) was placed in its original position before the entrance of the temple.

---

[31] **The gods of the Egyptians; or, studies in Egyptian Mythology. 2011 [Wikipedia]**

Asherah is very important to Canaanite and Hebrew theology. Both cultures are intertwined and important to Islamism. Asherah, or Ashtoreth, was the name of the chief female deity worshiped in ancient Syria, Phoenicia, and Canaan. The Phoenicians called her Astarte, the Assyrians worshiped her as Ishtar, and the Philistines had a temple of Asherah. Because of Israel's incomplete conquest of the land of Canaan, Asherah-worship survived and plagued Israel, starting as soon as Joshua was dead. Asherah is the origin of Easter. Considered the moon-goddess, Asherah was often presented as a consort of Baal, the sun-god. Asherah was also worshiped as the goddess of love and war and was sometimes linked with Anath, another Canaanite goddess. Worship of Asherah was noted for its sensuality and involved ritual prostitution. The priests and priestesses of Asherah also practiced divination and fortune-telling[32]. Asherah is also associated with the Hebrew god Yahweh. She is said to be the wife of Yahweh. The presence of Asherah or her symbol at places where Yahweh was worshipped raises the question of whether the Canaanite goddess was considered also to be the consort of Yahweh. Ishstar is also the origin of the Christian holiday Easter. The female counterpart is the polarity, duality or yin yang of

[32] **http://www.gotquestions.org/who-Asherah.html**

life.

Anthropologists have suggested that human culture began with the structuring of time and ritual, this was followed, much later, by regulation of weights and measures. The calendar preceded the measures, and we should not be surprised to find that the word mensuration is still in force to describe accurate measurement of quantity - length, areas, volume. From these are derived the weights. The root of this word, mens, relates directly to the moon, and we might inquire why this should be so. The modern sophisticated lifestyle, enjoyed within what has been described as a 'solar culture', latterly neglects the moon and is largely abstracted from any actual observations of the sky. As a consequence our technological culture finds difficulty in appreciating the role of an ancient sky watcher, even more so when it comes to reckon how their observations might have been recorded and subsequently analysed.

The study of the sky, stars, moon and sun is timeless. Since our early days as humans, we learned the internal workings of the galaxy.

Divination

The ancestors used instruments to communicate with different orishas/deities. According the Merriam Dictionary, divination is defined as:

> *Full Definition of DIVINATION*
> *1*
> *: the art or practice that seeks to foresee or foretell future events or discover hidden knowledge usually by the interpretation of omens or by the aid of supernatural powers*
>
> *2*
> *: unusual insight : intuitive perception*

Divination was used by the Indigenous people as scientific and mathematical method to communicate with the divine. Tehuti who is known as Hermes is called as the "word of god" or oracle.

Ifá is a religion and system of divination and refers to the verses of the literary corpus known as the Odu Ifá. Orunmila is identified as the Grand Priest, as he is who revealed divinity and prophecy to the world. Babalawo's use either the divining chain known as Opele, or the sacred palm or kola nuts called Ikin, on the wooden divination tray called Opon Ifá.

The Yoruba see the cosmos as divided into two halves of a sphere. In the upper half is orun, the world of the spiritual and the invisible – the deities, the ancestors, the various spirit forces. The lower half of the sphere is that of the visible tangible world in which we live, called the ase. Ifa divination creates the opportunity for communication between these two realms.

The process of Ifa divination is not a simple one. It is a complex system of numerical figures and infinite verses of memorized information. Ifa divination is based on interpreting sixteen basic numerical figures and 256 figures that can be derived from the original sixteen. These figures can be arrived at through two different processes. The first is through the manipulation of palm nuts. The diviner holds sixteen palm nuts in his left hand; with his right hand he grasps the nuts and if one is left, he puts two marks on his dining tray. If two nuts are left, he puts one mark on the tray. This process is repeated four times to give one of the sixteen combinations; repeating the process eight times gives one of the 256 derivative figures, called odus. The second, and quicker, method of obtaining the divination figures is by a single cast of a divining chain. The chain has eight seed shells attached and is held in the middle so that there are four shells on each side. The chain is then cast and the shells fall either face up or face down. A shell that has its concave surface upward is given a single mark. A concave surface downward is given a double mark (Bascom 3).

The basic sixteen figures of one and two marks are as follows:

OGBE OYEKU IWORI EDI OBARA OKANRAN IROSUN OWONRIN

I	II	II	I	I	II	
I	II					
I	II	I	II	II	II	
I	II					
I	II	I	II	II	II	
II	I					
I	II	II	I	II	I	
II	I					

OGUNDA   OSA   IRETE   OTURA   OTURUPON
IKA OSE OFUN

| I | | II | I | I | II | II |
| I | II | | | | | |

| I | | I | I | II | II | I |
| II | I | | | | | |

| I | | I | II | I | I | II |
| I | II | | | | | |

| II | | I | I | I | II | II |
| II | I | | | | | |

These sixteen basic figures can be paired in 256 ways (16 X 16). These 256 combinations are called the odus of Ifa divination. These are the possibilities that can be drawn on the Ifa tray by the diviner by either manipulating the palm nuts or casting the divining chain.

The Ifa diviner or priest is called a babalawo, father of ancient wisdom. The babalawo has memorized verses for each of the 256 odus. Most have learned at least four verses per odu and many diviners have memorized eight or more verses per odu, making their repertoire over 2000 verses, an incredible oral encyclopedia. The verses form the foundation of Yoruba tradition including folk tales, history, myths, songs, proverbs and riddles. The purpose of reciting these verses in the divination process is that one of the verses is Ifa's message related to the client's problem or inquiry. In this respect there is some discrepancy in how scholars perceive the relationship between client and diviner. William Bascom reports that many times the client does not even tell the diviner what his or her question or problem is, but instead whispers the information in cupped hands to a coin or other object which the diviner then touches with his divining chain to get the information to Ifa. The purpose of this is to get the information to the deity without the diviner being aware of the content. This makes certain there can be no chance of the diviner manipulating the odu and verse to what he thinks would be best. By keeping the inquiry secret the clients ensure communication directly between themselves and Ifa. The babalawo then recites all the verses he knows for the odu chosen and the clients select the verse relevant to their inquiry. In contradiction to this John Philip Neimark sees the role of the babalawo as more of a sacred counselor. He asserts that the true historical process was that the client confided in the diviner, and the babalawo used his deep social and psychological skills as well as his spiritual connections to guide the client to a solution to a problem. Neimark sees the role of the babalawo as one who tries to restore a sense of balance between the individual and the rest of the universe. The Yoruba see themselves as part of the larger organism which is the cosmos. Everything forms a piece of that cosmic being and in turn every part of the being contains particles of the whole. When we are in harmony with the energy of all, we are in balance. When we are out of balance with the universal, we suffer in many different ways. The role of divination and babalawo is to help maintain the balance of energy and to right any problems that may have arisen or might arise in the future.

The process of divination can be short and simple or very extended and complex as the following describes:

The general outline of the procedure in divination is as follows. (1) The first cast is made to determine the figure for which the verses are recited. (2) Two casts are made to determine whether the prognostication is for good or for evil. (3) Five casts are made to find out what kind of good or evil is indicated. (4) A succession of double casts may be made to find out in more detail about the evil. (5) Two casts are made to find out whether a sacrifice (ebo) is sufficient, or whether adimu [an additional sacrifice] is required. (6) If adimu is indicated, five casts are made to learn to whom it should be offered. (7) If adimu is to be made to a "white deity," it is identified by a succession of double casts. (8) Five casts are made to determine what is required as adimu. (9) If a live animal is required, a succession of double casts may be made to find out what kind. (10) The verses of the figure of the initial cast are recited, and the appropriate verse selected. (11) The correct sacrifice is determined by a succession of double casts. If at point five ebo is indicated, steps 6 through nine are omitted; and if the client wishes, steps 2 through 9 may be skipped, and if palm nuts are used, the process may be reduced to steps 1 and 10 only (Bascom 59).

The categories of good and evil the diviner ascertain are as follows: good – long life, money, wives and marriage, children, and victory over one's enemies; evil – death, sickness, fighting, the want of money, and loss (Bascom 55).

One of the babalawo's primary functions is to determine what the necessary sacrifice is to either ensure the client's good fortune or to moderate the evil fortune. If a sacrifice is called for, it is considered wise to make the sacrifices recommended as soon as possible. If the clients cannot afford the cost of the sacrifice or if they don't trust the babalawo, they simply might ignore the advice. In this case the only price is a small payment to the priest, which usually varies according to the individual's wealth. The diviner's main income is derived from sacrifices. If money is part of the sacrifice, it is understood that the diviner is to retain the money unless other specifications were given in the verses. In addition to or instead of money a great many other things can be included in the sacrifice: domestic animals, wild animals or meat, all kinds of food, implements, weapons, clothing and many other items could be specified in the verse. The diviner usually asks Ifa about the disposition of the sacrifice, what he can keep, how the meat of a sacrifice is to be shared in the community, if a hair might substitute for the animal, if a thread might substitute for a cloth, if a feather might substitute for a bird, and so on. In addition to prescribing sacrifices the babalawo, an accomplished herbalists, often calls for the preparations of magic or medicines known as ayajo. Common ingredients in these potions are the leaves of Ifa, some of the dust of the divining tray, and incantations (Bascom 61-5).

To become a babalawo is a long and difficult process requiring two very elaborate and expensive initiations. Instruction can start as early as the age of five or six with the student observing the babalawo performing his various duties and by beginning to learn the figures. Some diviners learn from their fathers while others are apprenticed to babalawo to learn the profession. The apprentice usually does not pay the master but serves him doing many duties and chores. Formal training can last from three to ten years with ongoing study continuing for life. The trainee studies with a babalawo learning the verses and the many rituals of the Ifa sect. Even after he is released from his teacher, he still owes an obligation to his teacher and may give the teacher a percent of his earnings for as long as the teacher lives. Many also continue learning verses for their entire lives, paying for the learning as they go (Bascom 81-6).

The babalawo has many duties beyond divination, including the many rituals and rites for those people who are specific followers of Ifa. One of the rites, Itefa, is a ritual for boys around the age of seven that guides them in finding their personal identity. It is series of rituals and symbolic journeys that are to lead to the child's rebirth at a new point in his life. The ceremony also empowers and prepares the initiate's personal set of palm nuts for Ifa divining. While the complexity of the series of rituals may be too sophisticated for the young boys to fathom at the time, it is a beginning of understanding that is reinforced many times as they observe and participate in the initiation of other boys. This learning process continues into adulthood. The components of the rites deal with hardships, joys, wealth, and creativity and take oral, visual, and kinetic modes of presentation. The learning process, both in the spiritual and material realms, relates new meanings to everyday life (Abiodun 178-88).

The Yoruba believe that a person's soul appears before Olorun in heaven before taking on a new human body and being given the opportunity to choose its destiny. Olorun may refuse if the requests are not made humbly or if they are unreasonable. The souls are given a fixed day they are to return to heaven, which cannot be altered except by suicide which prohibits the person from ever returning to heaven. If people gain the full support of their ancestral soul, Olorun, and their personal deity, they may live their allotted time on earth. If they are killed or die before their allotted time is over, they becomes ghosts here on earth

Ifa divination serves many functions in traditional Yoruba life but its primary function is to provide human beings with direct access to Olorun [Tehuti], who is in charge of their destinies. Ifa divination can give insight into what that destiny may be, what one's guardian ancestral soul is, which deity one should worship, what sacrifices are necessary to enhance one's destiny, what medicines are needed, and what evil might be working against one in the form of witches, evil spirits, curses and so on. While each individual has a personal deity to pray to, all people have access to the trinity of Olorun, Ifa, and Esu which controls their very destinies. The babalawo's verses also give guidance in matters of practical advice for living and moral and ethical behavior. Diviners are often consulted when people are in trouble, are about to undertake new ventures or travel, or have important decisions are to make. The destiny of a person defines the general boundaries of one's life: whether on will have good luck or bad luck, whether one will be wise or foolish, what one's occupation may be, how many children one will have, whether or not one will go insane, and so on. It can be said that Olorun determines the general direction of these factors in one's life, but the individual can do things to affect the extent of these conditions. One can divine and sacrifice to enhance good fortune and to mitigate bad fortune. If one is born with a "bad head," ancestral soul, he can try to lessen his bad conditions by right behavior and attention to the Gods and his ancestral soul (Bascom 117-8).

CHAPTER 8:

EATING THE INDIGENOUS WAY

One can not deal with an indigenous lifestyle without looking at the eating lifestyle. Living in a world filled with processed, fast foods and other foreign foods selection has a negative impact on our health physically and mentally. Melaninated people have a particular diet based on their environment. Our environment dictates the food design by nature. Consequently, most melaninated people originally lived where green leafy vegetables, fruits and nuts were readily available. This environment is in contrast to European climate which was cold and practically barren. This part of the book looks at foods indigenous to melaninted people here and Africa. It is fundamental for people to adopt a diet acceptable to your DNA. GMO's and high protein soul food must be abandoned. Let's look at some facts.

In a study conducted at the University of Pittsburgh, 20 African Americans and 20 South Africans switched diets for two weeks. In this time, the Africans consumed traditional American food meat and cheese high in fat content while African Americans took on a traditional African diet high in fiber and low in fat, with plenty of vegetables, beans and cornmeal, with little meat.

After the exchange, researchers performed colonoscopies on both groups and found that those in the African diet group increased the production of butyrate, a fatty acid proven to protect against colon cancer. Members of the American diet group, on the other hand, developed changes in their gut that scientists say precede the development of cancerous cells.

The diet of so called Africa Americans is a diet of disease and enslaved mentality. This is a major reason of the lower life expectancy among African Americans. Meat intake is much higher than traditional diet.

African Heritage Diet Pyramid
African Heritage Pyramid

Oldways has created the African Heritage Diet Pyramid with the help and knowledge of experts in African American and African Diasporan history, cuisine, nutrition, and public health. This healthy eating model was designed specifically for African Americans, and

African descendant populations everywhere, to introduce them to their Healthy Heritage. It can also be used by anyone wanting to use heritage as a guide to eating well. The Pyramid celebrates the individual foods and the traditional healthy eating patterns of African Heritage, with roots in America, Africa, the Caribbean, or South America.

Here are some foods found in Africa and Americas':

Central Africa were far less influenced by the European settlers. Centuries before the Europeans arrived, West African people were trading with the Arab world in spices and thus typically West African food is filled with hot spices. With the least contact with the "outside world", Central African food remains the closest to traditional ingredients and cooking techniques. The only notable adoption of cassava, peanut, and Chile pepper plants arrived along with the slave trade during the early 16th century.

Africa is a very fertile continent with a huge variety of food crop and fauna. During peace time, and with good rainfall, most communities are able to feed themselves just by farming at subsistence level - by means of small farms at the back of their homes or medium sized farms not far away from home. On the way back from farm, dinner could be a combination of:

Roasted yam and palm oil
Rice and fried plantain
Roasted plantain and home made sauce
Rice and tomatoes stew
Ga Kenkey[33]
Sweat potatoes and greens
Coconut and roasted or boiled maize
Pepper soup and boiled plantain or yam
Breadfruit and sauce
Fufu
Nshima
Koshari
Millet meal

Cruisine of the Americas

Native American cuisine includes all food practices of the indigenous peoples of the Americas. Modern-day native peoples retain a rich culture of traditional foods, some of which have become iconic of present-day Native American social gatherings (for example, frybread). Foods like cornbread, turkey, cranberry, blueberry,

---

[33] **Known as Kormi or Kokoe whih is a Sourdough dumpling from the Akan and Ewe of West Africa Served soup or sauce.**

hominy and mush are known to have been adopted into the cuisine of the United States from Native American groups. In other cases, documents from the early periods of contact with European, African, and Asian peoples allow the recovery of food practices which passed out of popularity.

The essential staple foods of the Eastern Woodlands Aboriginal Americans were maize (also called "corn"), beans, and squash. These were called the "Three Sisters" because they were planted interdependently: the beans grew up the tall stalks of the maize, while the squash spread out at the base of the three plants and provided protection and support for the root systems. A number of other domesticated crops were also popular during some time periods in the Eastern Woodlands, including a local version of quinoa, a variety of amaranth, sumpweed/marsh elder, little barley, maygrass, and sunflower.

The native populations of South America were cultivating an array of plants and developing strong irrigation systems before the Spanish discovered them. Starvation was never a worry for the Incans, because they preserved and stored many of their foods. South America is considered a global hub for genetic diversity of crops. Because of this, each region of South America has developed its own traditional foods. However, there are still tradition key ingredients in all South American cuisines.

Corn (Maiz): Corn has been cultivated in South America for more than 5,000 years and is a staple in dishes such as cornbread, corn tortillas, casseroles, and corn beer.
Potatoes: Rivaled only by corn, potatoes are another huge crop for South America and are fried, mashed, freeze dried, baked, and combined sauces to make many traditional dishes.

Peppers: Considered the most important seasoning of South american cooking, peppers come in both sweet and hot varieties and are used in a wide array of colorful dishes.

Tropical Fruit: Fruits such as coconuts, papayas, mango, guava, pineapple, passion fruit and more are considered staples and served with many meals.

Queso Fresco/Queso Blanco: Fresh cheese is another staple of South America. Queso fresco is often salted and added to sauces or crumbled on salads and sometimes eaten on biscuits.

Quinoa: Quinoa, the "mother seed," comes from a plant related to beets and spinach and contains all 9 amino acids essential for tissue development. It's often used to traditional soups.

At Estância Churrascaria, they serve traditional foods from the largest country in South America, Brazil. Our traditional sides include golden fried bananas, garlic mashed potatoes, polenta, rice and beans and homemade cheese bread rolls.

CHAPTER 9:
INDIGENOUS   HOLIDAYS   [AND   LUNAR
OBSERVATION]

Holiday's are special to various ethnic groups around the globe. Holiday's reflect the people and culture involved. The word holiday derives from two words holy day. Traditionally, a holiday comes from sacred holy days. It is important to install holiday's that reflect the indigenous cultures. These special days often originated with astrology. Many holidays come from the obervance of the sun. Look at traditional holidays in Africa and indigenous Americas'.

Chad
The Gerewol Festival

Each year the semi-nomadic Mbororo people gather for a week of incredible celebrations known as the Gerewol, a colourful festival that is one of Africa's most spectacular.

The Gerewol is renowned for the way in which young Mbororo men decorate themselves, donning make up and jewellery and 'displaying' to young women in search of a partner.

Ghana

Many festivals include thrilling durbars of chiefs, when tribal leaders and Queen Mothers process in decorated palanquins, shaded by the traditional umbrellas, and supported by drummers and warriors discharging ancient muskets. The dates of many festivals are determined by the traditional calendars, often decided close to the event.

Aboakyir festival - May each year

This Festival is celebrated by the people of Simpa or Winneba in the Central Region of Ghana. The festival is a celebration to mark the migration of these people from the ancient Western Sudan Empire where they were led by 2 brothers and a god called Otu. Upon consulting their god, they were instructed by their traditional priest or mediator between the people and the god to sacrifice a young member of the Royal family every year to their god.
Panafest

Panafest is a biennial festival of African dance, music and other performing arts that is held every two years in Ghana.   Panafest is a cultural event dedicated to the enhancement of the ideals of Pan-Africanism and the development of the African continent. It is organized biennially for Africans and people of Africa descent as well as all persons committed to the well being of

Africans on continent and in the diaspora. The essential thrust of PANAFEST is to enhance developement.

The Homowo Festival - August/September

African harvest festivals have a lot of religious significance. They are characterized by lots of dancing and singing. Dancers wear traditional masks and outfits. A popular dance sequence involves a good ghost who looks after their crops and scares away the bad ghosts who try to spoil the food.

Festival of Yams is a popular harvest festival celebrated with days of ceremonies and offerings to God and ancestors. Yams are the first crops to be harvested. People offer yams to the gods and ancestors first before they distribute them to the rest of the village.

The Homowo Festival of Africa, is a celebration of a traditional harvest festival from the Ga people of Ghana, West Africa, it is the largest cultural festival of its kind. For the Ga people, the word Homowo means "hooting at hunger."

The origin of Homowo is tied to the roots of the Ga people and their migration to Ghana. The Ga traveled for many years before reaching the west coast of Africa where they now live. Along the way they experienced famine, but through helping each other, they survived. Later when their harvests were plentiful, they held a feast at which they jeered and laughed at the hunger and hard times that had plagued them. This was the first Homowo.

The Homowo Festival begins with a traditional Ghanaian procession in which people assume the roles of kings, queens and followers of the royal family of each of Ghana's ethnic groups.

In some African cultures they hold a ceremony called "first fruits" [Similiar to Kwanzaa] that takes several days of planning in order to bless the newly harvested crops and purify the people before they eat the foods[34].

The Hogbetsotso Festival

This is celebrated on the first Saturday of November every year by the Anlo Ewes of the Volta Region of Ghana. The essential feature of this festival is a magnificent durbar of chiefs and citizens. Hogbetsotso, generally known as "the festival of the Exodus" is held annually to commemorate the escape of the Anlo Ewes from the tyrannical ruler of Notsie - Agokoli of Togo. The chiefs appear on the durbar grounds in their most

34 **Kwanzaa by Maulana Karenga**

charming royal regalia and sit in state to acknowledge and receive homage from their subjects. The entire ceremony is laced with non-stop soul-stirring drumming and dancing.

Holidays are opportunities to celebrate the Universe in a way that brings variety to our day-to-day practices. These holidays may differ from one Qadish to another, and may differ on the exact date that they are celebrated. Indeed, there exists very little information on any ancient Canaanite holiday. Much of the information we have is pieced together from crumbling tablets and filled in with poetry of the heart. A modern cycle of holidays, the Shanat Qadish or Sacred Year, might look something like this:

• Ashuru Mathbatu: Festival of Dwellings. This celebration marks the beginning of the year and occurs during the month of the autumnal equinox. It is called the Festival of Dwellings because the ancients would construct, on the temple rooftops, temporary housing from cut branches. Within these dwellings they would place statues or symbols of the Deities. (September-October, Autumnal Equinox).

• Ashuru Marzichu: At this time, we celebrate an annual gathering of a group, the Marzichu, dedicated to the veneration of the ancients and the Rapa'uma (deceased ancestors). The celebration features drinking rounds and a feast. (October-November, Full Moon).

• Ashuru Aru: Festival of Light. The festival of light centers around offerings of presentations (poetry, music, dance, storytelling, etc.). At this time, we venerate Shapshu, the Sun Goddess, and thank Her for spending time in the Underworld bringing Her light to our Rapa'uma. We gently remind Her that we, the living, also need Her light, and encourage Her with our presentations. (December-January, Winter Solstice).

• Ashuru Shamnu: Festival of Oil. The ancients, at this celebration, made a libation of the "Oil of Well-being," and would make prayers to Baal for protection of the city-state. This is an excellent holiday to make anointing oils: the ancients had an oil scented with myrrh, and an oil perfumed with spices. (January-February, Seventh day after the New Moon).19

• Ashuru Gannu: Festival of the Garden. It's time to celebrate spring! One of the ancient rites involved sitting in a garden and partaking of fish soup. Perhaps this would help encourage the growth and abundance of the garden, or perhaps it's just an excellent time for a picnic. (March-April, Vernal Equinox)

• Ashuru Liyatu: Festival of Garlands. It is time to celebrate the abundance of the first harvest. Almonds and figs have come into season. This is a feasting celebration. (May-June, Full Moon)

• Ashuru Zabru: Festival of Pruning. It's time to prune the grapevines, and by extension, sympathetic magic to prune the influences of Mot during the hot summer season. Also, we celebrate the birth of the twin Gods, Shachar and Shalim. (June-July, Summer Solstice).

• Ashuru Ra'shu Yeni: Festival of New Wine. At the new moon, the ancients would make an offering of a bunch of grapes to El. The actual festival would begin just before the full moon and carry on for several days. This is a celebration of fun, frolic, and fertility to celebrate the successful grape harvest. (Festival of New Wine: New Moon and Full Moon).23

Dogons Festivals

The Dogons are famous for their masks and during the five-day event many of them are used in ritual ceremonies that go back more than 1000 years . At each Sigui festival, a new ceremonial mask is carved especially for the occasion, then placed in the Tellem caves. Remnants of these masks going back hundreds of years have been found in the caves.

Crossing of the cattle - December

The Cattle Crossing is the most important Fulani festival in Diafarabe. Every December, herders bring cattle from the grazing lands to the river at Diafarabe. Here everyone crosses the river. On the other side families are reunited for a few days, before they take the cattle to new pastures. The first day is the Promenade des Jeunes, when the unmarried men and women dress up to attract each other. There is also a competition to judge the fattest and best looked-after cattle, with useful prizes.

Nigeria
Durbar Festival - Oct

The Durbar festival is celebrated at the culmination of the two great Muslim festivals Id el Fitri and Id el Kabir. The festival gives a good idea of the past glories of the emirate before the influence of western culture.

Tanzania
The Wildebeest Migration

The Wildebeest Migration in East Africa, also known as "The Great Migration" takes place between Tanzania's Serengeti National Park and Kenya's Masai Mara and is one of the greatest wildlife spectacles on the planet.

Thousands of wildebeest and zebra's migrate between the Serengeti and the Masai Mara, constantly driven by their search for fresh grazing. The massive herds are closely followed by predators (lion, hyena and cheetah), making the most of every opportunity to catch their next meal.

The precise timing of the annual wildebeest migration depends on the rains. It is a very unpredictable and spontaneous natural event, with calving season taking place in the Serengeti between January and mid-March. The wildebeest migration starts to head towards the Western Serengeti in May or June. The best time to see the migration is generally between June and August when the wildebeest congregate and prepare to cross the famous Grumeti River.

If you are in the Masai Mara you can expect the wildebeest to make their arrival as early as July, but they generally arrive between August & September and remain in the Masai Mara between October & November. Between the end of November and January the wildebeest gradually begin their migration from the Masai Mara back towards the Serengeti.

This safari allows you to witness the very best of Tanzania. You will revel in all the wildlife viewing opportunities on the fabled plains of the Serengeti, around

Uganda
Bayimba International Festival of Music and Arts

The Annual Bayimba International Festival of Music and Arts – a vibrant platform to celebrate the power of Music and Arts in Uganda.

Zanzibar
Sauti za Busara music festival

Features a rich variety of African music from the region with more than four hundred musicians participating over five days in historic Stone Town.
Festival of the Dhow Countries July

East Africa's largest cultural event, takes place in Zanzibar in magnificent, historical venues along the waterfront of Stone Town. The festival celebrates the unique cultural heritage of the "Dhow" countries: the African continent and the Indian Ocean region and their global Diaspora.

Mwakakogwa Festival - July/August

A traditional festival to celebrate the local New Year. It is mainly practiced in the Southern Unguja[35] particularly in Makunduchi. Originating from Persia and brought here by early, Immigrants, Mwakakogwa is marked by sacrifices, dances, and the actual field fighting. In addition to the tourists from abroad, it draws participants from the whole of East Africa.

---

[35] **On the island of Tanzania**

Kemet [Nubia]

Abu Simbel is located in the heart of Nubia and is accessible by road or air from Aswan. The most remarkable feature of the site is that the temple is precisely oriented so that twice every year, on 22 February and 22 October, the first rays of the morning sun shine down the entire length of the temple-cave to illuminate the back wall of the innermost shrine and the statues of the four gods seated there.

Ramses II, in a fit of precision and despotic architectural egotism, carefully angled his temple at Abu Simbel so that the inner sanctum would light up twice a year: once on the anniversary of his rise to the throne, and once on his birthday. The combination of human endeavour and natural phenomena provides what must be one of the most spectacular sights in the world.

Ethiopia
Timkat/Epiphany - January

Timket, or the Feast of the Epiphany, is celebrated in the January of each year. The 3-day event commemorates the baptism of Christ and is one of the most colourful Ethiopian festivals. The night before the Timket, priests take the Tabot (which symbolises the Ark of the

Covenant, containing the Ten Commandments) from each church to a tent at a consecrated pool or stream. There is frenetic activity, including the ringing of bells, blowing of trumpets and the burning of incense. In Addis Ababa, tents are pitched at Jan Meda, to the northeast of the city centre. At 02:00am, mass is celebrated, attended by crowds of people carrying lighted oil lamps. At dawn, the priest uses a ceremonial cross to extinguish a candle burning on a pole in a nearby river. Inevitably, some of the congregation leap into the river. The Tabots are then taken back to the churches in procession, accompanied by horsemen, while the festivities continue.

Cape Town Festival

The Festival will include concerts over three days, our popular Festival Imbizos or Cultural Talks, diverse foods representing different religions and cultures, and a range of activities targeting youth, etc.

Hermanus Whale Festival

The fun Festival with the most spectacular natural setting on earth brings you a combination of music, music, music, live theatre, sport and adventurous environmental activities - the ultimate Enviro-Arts experience. A whole week of theatre, music, craft stalls, sport and fun is planned - bring the whole family.

Absa Cape Epic
Mauritus New Year

A spectacular event, and a deeply symbolic one. In Mauritius it is treated as a spring cleaning both of the inner and the outer worlds, as families get together to celebrate the beginning of a new year with vows, fireworks, good food and celebration.
africa travel.

Kwanzaa

As an melaninated American and Pan-African holiday celebrated by millions throughout the world African community, Kwanzaa brings a cultural message which speaks to the best of what it means to be African and human in the fullest sense. Given the profound significance Kwanzaa has for African Americans and indeed, the world African community, it is imperative that an authoritative source and site be made available to give an accurate and expansive account of its origins, concepts, values, symbols and practice.

Moreover, given the continued rapid growth of Kwanzaa and the parallel expanded discussion of it and related issues, an authoritative source which aids in both framing and informing the discussion is likewise of the greatest importance. Therefore, the central interest of this website is to provide information which reveals and reaffirms the integrity, beauty and expansive meaning of the holiday and thus aids in our approaching it with the depth of thought, dignity, and sense of specialness it deserves.

The holiday, then will of necessity, be engaged as an ancient and living cultural tradition which reflects the best of African thought and practice in its reaffirmation of the dignity of the human person in community and culture, the well-being of family and community, the integrity of the environment and our kinship with it, and the rich resource and meaning of a people's culture.

Juneteenth

Officially, the Emancipation Proclamation freed "all persons held as slaves within any State or designated part of a State" where the residents were "in rebellion against the United States." In practice, it applied only to those slaves who lived near Union lines, where they could make an easy escape or take advantage of the Northern advance.

News of emancipation would move slowly, which would be compounded by the mass migration of slave owners, who fled their holdings in Louisiana and Mississippi slaves in tow following the Union victories at New Orleans in 1862 and Vicksburg in the spring and summer of 1863. Tens of thousands of slaves arrived in Texas, joining the hundreds of thousands in the interior of the state, where they were isolated from most fighting and any news of the war. Indeed, Union attempts to occupy Texas were limited to the coastlines far from the densest slave populations or repelled before they had a chance to succeed.

Gye Nyame

Gye Nyame (the new-African cultural holiday alternative to Thanksgiving) was first celebrated by a group of nearly 500 Pan African-Nationalists. Egbe Gye Nyame, a small, yet powerful and dedicated African centered study group joined and supported the late Dr. Khallid Abdul Muhammad, founder and creator of Gye Nyame, in preparing for this historic, monumental and most auspicious occasion. Dr. Khallid's young thirteen year old son, Farrakhan Khallid Muhammad lit the Gye Nyame Candle for the first holiday celebration. The sacred and solemn theme chosen for this day was "On This Day We

Give Thanks To The One God And To Our Ancestors". And it was decided that this theme would follow throughout the years.

It was November, 1995, in New York City [Harlem] that Gye Nyame was created and designed for melaninated people in America. Later it was at the invitation of the young activist attorney Malik Zulu Shabazz of Howard University in Washington D.C. that Dr. Khallid originally announced its coming celebration. It was first widely shared in interviews with the Hip Hop/ Rap magazine Source, XXL magazine, The Alarm in London and The Daily Challenge [New York's only Black daily newspaper].

Gye Nyame is celebrated every year on the third Thursday of November (the same day that the "American Thanksgiving" holiday is celebrated). African culture, spirituality, ritual, ceremony and symbology is all over Gye Nyame and is taken from all over Africa.

Though it is officially a one day celebration, the spirit of Gye Nyame must be carried on throughout the year.

Like Kwanzaa [created by Dr. Maulana Karenga in December of 1966], Gye Nyame follows and joins in a celebration of self and the celebrating of that which is in our own image and interest.

Like Kwanzaa (celebrated December 26th - January 1st), Gye Nyame is not to be seen as "just a reactionary reflex" to the holidays of others. Gye Nyame is "a self-conscious cultural choice". It offers an opportunity for a serious, clear and compelling choice. We have no other "real" or "realistic" choice. For the only way to fight and successfully defeat an imposed, oppressive alien culture is to live our own with self-affirming focus, commitment, purpose and pride.

Moorish American Week

This week honors Noble Drew Ali starting on his born day of January 8th through 15th. The week recognises Moorish Americans, indigenous people and the celebration of the works of Prophet Noble Drew Ali. The end of the week starts the Moorish American new year.

Indigenous American Holidays

The Sun Dance associated colors are red, yellow, white and black. The colors represent the following:

Red = the sunset
Yellow = forked lightning
White = light
Black = night

This dance is observed in late June or early July, wherever the first full moon closest to the summer solstice lands. The Sioux aren't the only tribe that performed this dance. It's also performed by the: Arapaho, Arikara, Asbinboine, Blackfoot, Bungi, Comanche, Cheyenne, Crow, Gros, Ventre, Hidutsa, Sioux, Plains Cree, Plains Ojibway, Sarasi, Omaha, Ponca, Ute, Shoshone, Mandan, and Kiowa, tribes. As with all cultures, the Native Americans also feel that seasonal and celestial cycles are important to them, mostly because they migrated so much in their past.

The ceremony lasts 16 days. The first 8 days are spent in preparation. The performance is 4 days. Then 4 days of abstinence. This is a time for renewal and healing. They feel it was crucial this ceremony be held at midsummer when the sage plant was succulent and when the sun was at it's highest point in the sky.

The participants of the dance fasted (not eating or drinking) during the actual dance. They'd take a sweat bath in the morning on the first day. Then they'd paint their bodies in the symbolic colors mentioned above. They'd dress in a deerskin apron and wristlets. They wore anklets made of rabbit's fur. And, they had a feather in their hair. Members from tribes many miles away would come and set up their teepees to form a circular dance area around the sun pole. This sun pole had been cut and painted in advance. The music accompaniment of the Sun Dance is a large drum, along with ceremonial songs. The dancers will circle in procession as a way of communing with the creator, the sun and the earth.

Soyal, Soyala, Sol-ya-lang-eu

The date of this observation is on December 22. It is celebrated by the Hopi Indians. Although a black Plumed Snake is the basic symbol of this ceremony. But it is not based on snake worship. [Just like the Snake Dance Ceremony] It is a ceremony related to the sun as it relates to the winter solstice. It is one of the Hopi's most sacred ceremonies and is also called the "Prayer-Offering Ceremony" because it is a time for saying prayers for the New Year and for wishing each other prosperity and health.

Worshiping the sun is pretty common among many ancient people. In North America, the Hopi also noticed that the sun rose and set at different points on the horizon.

They also noticed that the sun would reach it's most vertical position in the summer and that when the sun rose lower in the sky it meant that the weather was colder and the earth was barren.

In midsummer, the Hopi performed their Snake Dance Ceremony when they felt the sun was close to the earth. Basically the Sun Dance was a request for rain from the gods of the underworld. When the sun started to go away, the Hopi attention was now focused on the sun leaving them altogether.

The Hopi believed that at the winter solstice that took place in December the Sun God had traveled as far from the earth as he ever did. So, in order to bring the Sun God back, this meant that it would require the most powerful humans to talk the Sun God to turn around and come back to them.

Therefore, the whole purpose of the Soyaluna ceremony that the Hopi do still to this day, is to prevent the disappearance of the sun at the time of the year when the days are the shortest.

Lunar Observation

The moon has always been a sign to indigenous people for centuries. Lunar cycles have an impact on our daily lives. New and full moons are used to influence human affairs. Many rituals are conducted during full and new moons. New moons are when the moon is not visible. The new moon has no reflection therefore it appears there is no moon. This symbolizes a new start and new month.

CHAPTER 10:
JURISDICTION, AFFIDAVITS AND TRUSTS

How do we live indigenous in this society? It seems the State has all the laws in place for everyone. This part of the book will assist indigenous people how to protect all cultural, spiritual and indigenous rights granted by The Rights of Indigenous People, Treaty of Peace and Friendship w/ Morocco 1787 and Universal Declaration of Human Rights. Jurisdiction is very important in maintaining indigenous status and lifestyle. Jurisdiction is a multi faceted word. It is not the same terminology used by so called Sovereign Citizens or any other groups. Jurisdiction deals with contracts in the form of affidavits. Affidavits are the primary legal document used by indigenous people to secure their jurisdiction and rights.

The definition of jurisdiction is:

Power of a court to adjudicate cases and issue orders. Territory within which a court or government agency may properly exercise its power.See, e.g. Ruhrgas AG v. Marathon Oil Co. et al., 526 U.S. 574 (1999).

jurisdiction: an overview

One of the most fundamental questions of law is whether a given court has jurisdiction to preside over a given case. A jurisdictional question may be broken down into three components:

whether there is jurisdiction over the person (in personam), whether there is jurisdiction over the subject matter, or res (in rem), and whether there is jurisdiction to render the particular judgment sought. The term jurisdiction is really synonymous with the word "power". Any court possesses jurisdiction over matters only to the extent granted to it by the Constitution, or legislation of the sovereignty on behalf of which it functions. The question of whether a given court has the power to determine a jurisdictional question is itself a jurisdictional question. Such a legal question is referred to as "jurisdiction to determine jurisdiction."

Subject matter jurisdiction is the court's authority to decide the issue in controversy such as a contracts issue, or a civil rights issue. State courts have general jurisdiction, meaning that they can hear any controversy except those prohibited by state law (some states, for example, deny subject matter jurisdiction for a case that does not involve state citizens and did not take place in the state) and those allocated to federal courts of exclusive jurisdiction such as bankruptcy issues (see 28 U.S.C. § 1334). Federal courts have limited jurisdiction in that they can only hear cases that fall both within the scope defined by the Constitution in Article III Section 2 and Congressional statutes (See 28 U.S.C. §1251, §1253, §1331, §1332).

Territorial jurisdiction is the court's power to bind the parties to the action. This law determines the scope of federal and state court power. State court territorial jurisdiction is determined by the Due Process Clause of the Constitution's Fourteenth Amendment and the federal court territorial jurisdiction is determined by the Due Process Clause of the Constitution's Fifth Amendment.

Other forms of jurisdiction include appellate jurisdiction (the power of one court to correct the errors of another, lower court), concurrent jurisdiction (the notion that two courts might share the power to hear cases of the same type, arising in the same place), and diversity jurisdiction (the power of Federal courts to hear cases in which the parties are from different states). An example showing the interplay of diversity jurisdiction with subject-matter jurisdiction is Grupo Dataflux v. Atlas Global Group, L. P. (02-1689), 541 U.S. 567 (2004)[36].

---

[36] Holidays, Symbols & Customs 3rd Edition" By Sue Ellen Thompson Om

Affidavits were mentioned earlier to be used to replace contracts, licenses and certificates. This is the definition of Affidavits:

An affidavit is a written statement that is confirmed by the oath or affirmation of the party making it before a person authorised to receive affidavits. Affidavits are used in court proceedings and for other purposes authorised by law.

When you complete an affidavit you are given a choice to make an affirmation or to swear an oath.

An affidavit must be used to create a personal jurisdiction within the jurisdiction of the State. It is a way to bypass State jurisdiction because it cuts out the need for a judge in most cases. For example, a Marriage Affidavit does not need a Probate judge to give permission to marry in the state. It also allows a spiritual leader to marry without being licensed to the state.

Here are the common affidavits needed in our indigenous society:

Affidavit of Common Law Marriage

nigraphics, Inc. © 2003.

Affidavit of Live Birth
Affidavit of Nationality and Indigenous Status
Affidavit of Automobile Ownership
Affidavit of Financial Responsibility
Affidavit of Deceased
Affidavit of Right to Travel
Affidavit of Vaccination Exemption

Taxes exempt status is another benefit of Indigenous peoples. Under Title 22 FOREIGN RELATIONS AND INTERCOURSE page 954 Chapter 2: Consular courts. Certificate Registration numbers AA 77869, AA 209316 and AA 222141[37].

These affidavits and others are used to create a record

your affirmed statements and oath. Your affidavits should be filed with the County Recorder office or Clerk of Courts. This action puts your affidavits on the county record which is also public record. Many of these affidavits are also contractual with other parties [wife, mother of child] involved. These affidavits create their own jurisdiction. For example, an affidavit of Live Birth creates a contract between the mother, father and child that determines the existence of a baby, the names, status

---

[37]**Is there Thanksgiving in Africa? Author: Wayne**

of parents and custodial rights. You create your rights and your status instead of receiving the documents [contracts] from the government. Signing government and quasi governmental agencies contracts creates a jurisdiction that makes you liable. These agreements are perceived as voluntary servitude. Indigenous African, melaninated and Moorish have human rights because we are the true people of this planet. For more information refer to the book *Moors, Moabite and Man*. The next issue is how to protect your money

What Is a Trust Fund?

To understand how a trust fund works, let's look at an example. You've worked hard all of your life and built up a comfortable savings cushion. You know that sometime in the future you're going to pass away, and you want your hard-earned savings to go to the people you love, or the charities or causes that you believe in.

Now, what about loved ones who are not as financially savvy as you? You could be concerned about leaving them a lump sum gift because they might use it irresponsibly. Furthermore, you may even like to see your money carry over for generations to come. If this is how you feel, then you should set up a living irrevocable trust fund. This type of trust can be set up to begin dispersing funds when certain conditions are met. There is no stipulation that you cannot be alive when that happens.

You can place cash, stock, real estate or other valuable assets in your trust. You meet with an attorney and decide on the beneficiaries and set stipulations. Maybe you say that the beneficiaries receive a monthly payment, can only use the funds for education expenses, expenses due to an injury or disability, or the purchase of a first home. It's your money so you get to decide.

Because it's irrevocable, you don't have the option of later dissolving the trust fund. Once you place assets in the trust, they are no longer yours. They are under the care of a trustee. A trustee is a bank, attorney or other entity set up for this purpose.

Since the assets are no longer yours, you don't have to pay income tax on any money made from the assets. Also, with proper planning, the assets can be exempt from estate and gift taxes. These tax exemptions are a primary reason that some people set up an irrevocable trust. If you, the trustor (the person setting up the trust) is in a higher income tax bracket, setting up the irrevocable trust allows you to remove these assets from your net worth and move in to a lower tax bracket.

Traditional trust funds have long been used by high net-worth families, but even those with very little money can easily set up an irrevocable trust. The **Kiss** Trust is a product with lower net worth individuals in mind. It has all of the advantages of a traditional trust, it's inexpensive to set up, and you can start the trust with as much money as it would take to buy a tank of gas. You can make a lump sum deposit or deposit regular amounts. The Kiss Trust is safe from taxes, bankruptcy and divorce. Finally, for a family who would like to set up a trust for more than one person can contribute to it, the Kiss Trust allows for an infinite amount of people to become trustors.

As you have read, a trust can protect you and your family. It is a powerful tool that can be used to separate indigenous people from the State. Use the trust to operate in commerce or to put property [houses, cars, paychecks etc]. Trusts create their own jurisdiction that allows protection from different corporate fictions. There are many different trusts however, the Kiss Trust can be applied by all indigenous people because it's inexpensive and easy to complete without a lawyer.

APPENDIX

APPENDIX 1
RITES OF PASSAGE

CHART 1
AFRICENTRIC RITES OF PASSAGE: A CHANGE MODEL FOR VALUES, ATTITUDES, AND BEHAVIORS AMONG AFRICAN AMERICAN YOUTH

INDEPENDENT VARIABLE:
AFRICENTRIC RITES OF PASSAGE
*Worldview
*Value System
*Socialization Process

Nguzo Nane (Eight Principles)

1. Unity
2. Self-Determination
3. Collective Work and
   Responsibility
4. Cooperative Economics

5. Purpose
6. Creativity
7. Faith
8. Respect

INTERVENING VARIABLES: VALUES/ATTITUDES

1. Belief in Supreme Being/Spirituality
2. Sense of Manhood/Womanhood
3. Increased Self Esteem
4. Higher Expectations for Future Success
5. Belief in Cooperative Ethic
6. Increased Respect for Others
7. Greater sense of community identity/commitment

DEPENDENT VARIABLES: RESPONSIBLE BEHAVIORS

1. Development of career plans
2. Proper nutrition/exercise
3. Safe sexual behavior
4. Increased stress management
5. Increased problem solving skills
6. Increased conflict resolution skills
7. Increased positive relationships with parents, peers, teachers, and elders
8. Increased community service

APPENDIX: 2
MARRIAGE AFFIDAVIT

FOR RECORDER PURPOSES ONLY

Moorish American Affidavit of Marriage

Temple of New Kemit, Warren County, Al Moroc (America): **Ohio**

I, *HUSBANDS NAME* and *WIFE MAIDEN NAME*, both being *the age of majority* and after first being duly cautioned and affirmed, state the following:

1. 𝒲e share the same regular and permanent residence.

2. 𝒲e are Moorish American Free Nationals in *Sui Juris* and *Propia Personam*.

3. 𝒲e are domiciled in united states of America (Al Moroc), Republic, Moorish Republic New

Kemit; Montgomery County, Ohio.

4. 𝔅oth parties mutually consent and agree to be married as husband and wife as given by the

Moorish American National Sovereigns 1928.

5. 𝒲e are not relatives by blood, ancestor or adoption.

6. 𝒲e are aware of no facts or circumstances that would prevent our marriage from being recognized under Moorish, U.S. Constitutional and *Common* laws. **This affidavit is void if any marriage, by either party not lawfully terminated by death, divorce or dissolution.**

7. 𝒲e take on the Moorish Free National names of:
HUSBANDS NAME, and *WIFE'S MARRIED NAME*, as husband and wife and recognized as such in the Moorish/African community and County in which we *domicile*.

8. 𝒲e certify under penalty of perjury, under laws of the United States and Moorish Republic, the foregoing is true and correct. All unalienable Rights Reserved.

OFFICIAL USE ONLY

_____   _____

Husband's Signature in *Sui Juris*   Wife's Signature in *Sui Juris*

_____   _____

Witness 1   Witness 2

_____   _____2016

Notary Public Signature   Date

_____   _____2016

Signature of Person Solemnizing or performing Marriage   Date

_____
Title: (Religious/Civil)
Please Print

_____

Authorized Moorish Officer's signature in *Sui Juris*

APPENDIX 3
INDIGENOUS AFFIDAVIT OF LIVE BIRTH
FOR RECORDER PURPOSES ONLY

Indigenous Affidavit of Live Birth

New Kemit, Montgomery County, Al Moroc (America): Ohio

I, *Aylissa Renae Hopkins [Amrah Janan El]* and *Markell Gabrielle Reed [Ouran Abdul Aameen Ras Nyahbinghi El Bey]*, both being *the age of majority,* sound mind and body and after first being duly affirmed, state the following:

1. *O*ur child's name (title) is *Jibrill Mikail Isafril Malak Aameen El Bey* , who was manifested on February 22nd , 2015 at 3:23 p.m. Eastern Standard Time.
2. *We* mutually consent and agree both to being natural custodial and paternal parents of **Jibrill Mikail Isafril Malak Aameen El Bey.**
3. *We* are Indigenous American Free Nationals in *Sui Juris* and *Propia Personam.*
4. *We* are domiciled in united states of America (Al Moroc), Republic, Moorish Republic New Kemit; Hamilton County, Ohio.
5. *J*ibrill Mikail Isafril Malak Aameen El Bey is a Indigenous American (Muracano) free National child domiciled in the united states of America (Al-Moroc), Republic,New Kemit; Hamilton County, Ohio.
6. *We* declare *"sui juris"* status in connection to our names, property and offspring (children). If any agency of the said government disputes the declaration of *"sui juris",* in connection with the name's sworn and sealed in the affidavit. I demand a certified copy with signed authorization of all contracts and documents "held-in-due-course," pursuant to UCC 3-505.2, UCC 3-305.52 and UCC 3-505. **WE EXPLICITLY RESERVE ALL UNALIENABLE RIGHTS WITHOUT PREJUDICE** pursuant to UCC 1-308 O.R.C. 1301.13 and UCC 1-103.6.
7. *We* certify under penalty of perjury, under laws of the United States and Moorish New Kemit Republic, the foregoing is true and correct.

_____   _____
Custodial Father's Signature in *Sui Juris*   Custodial Mother's Signature in *Sui Juris*

_____   _____
Witness for Father   Witness for Mother

_____   _____2015
Notary Public Signature   Date

_____
Authorized Moorish Official signature in *Sui Juris*

APPENDIX 4
AUTOMOBILE AFFIDAVIT

MOORISH REPUBLIC OF NEW KEMIT- MONTGOMERY COUNTY, OHIO

AFFIDAVIT OF AUTOMOBILE OWNERSHIP/COMMON LAW REGISTRATION/PLATES

OWNER(S) NAME: Endisha Adilia El Bey   **AUTOMOBILE YEAR: 1999**

TYPE OF AUTOMOBLIE: 4 DOOR SUV   **CLASS: NON-COMMERCIAL**

ODOMETER READING: 70,912   **MAKE: FORD**

AUTOMOBILE SERIAL NO.: 1FMRU123XXXX   **PURCHASE DATE: 03/10/2006**

- I am a Moorish national and indigenous to America (Al-Moroc).
- I am a citizen of The Moorish Republic of New Kemit Community.
- This automobile is not a motor vehicle or used for commercial purposes.
- This automobile is covered with insurance or bond.
- I am the owner and of this automobile.
- The information provided is true and an accurate record to the best of my knowledge.
- I declare *sui juris* on my property and automobile.
- All rights reserved pursuant to O.R.C. 1301.13 and 1301.308.
- I reserve the right to travel on all public highways and byways.

_____   _____ 2016

Owner signature in Sui Juris   Date

_____   _____ 2016

Notary Public Signature   Date

_____

Authorized Moorish Officer Signature   SEAL

APPENDIX: 5
IMMUNIZATION LETTER TO SCHOOL

(JANUARY 8, 2016)

(Address to your local Board of Education)

§3313.671 - Required Immunizations; Exceptions

B.4 – A pupil who presents a written statement of the pupil's parent or guardian in which the parent or guardian objects to the immunization for good cause, including religious convictions, is not required to be immunized.

To Whom It May Concern:

    I am a Moorish-American, indigenous person and after listening to many debates; reading a variety of articles, facts, and personal accounts; and personally interviewing numerous authorities on either side of the vaccine issue, I have decided that vaccines are not in the best interest of my child,

_____.

    Thank you,

APPENDIX 6:
AFFIDAVIT FOR SUPPORT OF CHILD

I, <u>Dr. Shabazz El</u>, custodial parent of <u>Michelle El</u>, resident of 1514, Davis Drive, Faith Avenue, Atlanta, Georgia, do hereby solemnly swear and declare as under:

1. That my citizenship/nationality is Moorish. My county recorder number is ABC1234 issued in Montgomery County on September 14th 2008.

2. That I am employed as/in business Medical Professional since December 1995 and my annual income is $200000 as per last check stub of year.

3. That I am supporting my son/daughter, <u>Michelle El</u>, resident of 1514, Davis Drive, Faith Avenue, Atlanta, Georgia, who is 7 year old and is a minor.

4. My child support extends till age 18 or emancipted, beginning from September 2012 to July 2023. That I undertake to provide full/partial financial support till the age of 18 or emanicapation, including his/her medical fees.

_____   _____
   Custodial Father signature   Custodial Mother signature

                          2016
_____ _____
   Notary Pubic Signature   Date

_____
Office of Temple of New Kemit signature

134

APPENDIX 7
AFFIDAVIT OF DOMICILE FOR DEATH OF SPOUSE/CHILD/OTHER

AFFIDAVIT OF DOMICILE

STATE OF_____)

)SS: COUNTY OF_____)

_____, being duly sworn deposes and says that he/she

non resident at _____, State of

_____ and is executor/administrator of the estate of

_____ deceased, who died on the _____ day of_____

20_____; at the time of his/her death the domicile (legal residence) of said decedent was

_____,

(address)

County of _____, State of _____ for _____ years

prior to death, and was not a resident of any other State (other than that of his/her domicile) within the

United States of America, at the time of death.

This affidavit is made for the purpose of securing the transfer or delivery of securities registered in the

name of or owned by said decedent at the time of his/her death.

_____ (EXECUTOR/ADMINISTRATOR/SURVIVOR/HEIR)

Subscribed and sworn to before me

this _____ day of _____, 20_____ _____ (NOTARY PUBLIC)

My commission Expires _____

--AUTHORIZED MOORISH OFFICIAL ONLY----------------------------

_____

Office of Moorish Temple of New Kemit signature

APPENDIX 8:

AFFIDAVIT OF DEATH

RECORDING REQUESTED BY:
AND WHEN RECORDED MAIL TO:
SPACE ABOVE THIS LINE IS FOR RECORDER'S USE

AFFIDAVIT - DEATH

STATE OF OHIO } COUNTY OF MONTGOMERY}

OF LEGAL AGE, BEING FIRST DULY SWORN, DEPOSES AND SAYS: That , the decedent mentioned in the attached certified copy of Certificate of Death, is the same person as , named as one of the parties in that certain dated , execute
Date:

I, _____ , at _____ , _____ (State), hereby certify that the following natural person

Name _____ Sex _____ Date of Birth_____2016

Age _____ Eye Color _____

has been disposed of as follows:

Died or was killed on _____, 2016

at this address _____

on _____, 2016

_____
Signed by physician, coroner or authorized person

SUBSCRIBED AND SWORN TO BEFORE ME
THIS _____ DAY OF _____, 2016
Signature of Notary Public
Notary Public Commissioned for said County and State

--------------------------------------AUTHORIZED MOORISH OFFICIAL--------------------------------------

_____
Officer of Moorish Temple of New Kemit

APPENDIX 9

TAX EXEMPT STATUS INDIGENOUS

This is an example of a Moorish Indigenous Natural person being tax - exempt. Notice the use of AA 222-141. With your nationality card and tax exempt number, you have the ability to become a tax free on purchases. This number is considered by many as a diplomatic registration however it is a number for NON PROFIT TAX EXEMPT. Please be advised that this is not to be used for diplomatic purpose.

APPENDIX 10
KEMETIC CALENDAR

THE TIME IS NOW... THE YEAR IS 6256 K.A. (KEMETIC ALMANAC)			
Agri-Cycle	Kemetic		Gregorian
Akhet Harvest	Tehuti	1	January
	MenKhet	2	Febuary
	HetHeru	3	March
	Renutt	4	April
Shemu Inundation	ShefBdet	5	May
	Rekh-Nedjs	6	June
	Rekh-Wr	7	July
	Ka-Her-Ka	8	August
Pert Planting Seeds	Khenti-Kheti	9	September
	Khonsu	10	October
	Ipet	11	November
	Mes-Ra	12	December
	Wep Renpet		5 Days Over
NOT 2015 A.D. (AFTER THE DECEPTION)... REMEMBER THE TIME			

This picture expresses the evidence of indigenous people creating in Kemet a calendar system which pre dates Greek, Roman and any other so called European dating systems. This is a link back to a time when the ancestors used their own time. It is very important for indigenous people to adapt indigenous concepts of time and incorporate this into the modern calendar. This can be used to re estabish our time and year like other culture.

APPENDIX 11

MELANINATED PEOPLE AROUND THE WORLD: AZTECS

19th Century Portrait of an Aztec Couple. Hulton-Deutsch Collection, Getty images

This is one of the last portaits of an Aztec. The Aztecs were a great civilization prior to European exploration and conquest of Central America. Their features are very similiar to Africanoid.

APPENDIX 11 CONTINUED
OCEANIC PEOPLE

This picture displays the characteristics of Oceanic People of the globe in 1894. The true definition identifies them as indigenous people which include Pacific Island [Polynesian, Melanesian and Micronesian] also include Chamorros of Guam, Hawaii and Marshall Islands. Many others are Australia, Papua New Guinea, New Zealand [Maori].

APPENDIX 11 CONTINUED
FIJIANS

Here is another picture of melninated oceanic peoples of Fijians and Tongans. The afro is a universal symbol of indigenous people across the globe. These people are known to arrived from Melanesia around 3,500 years ago. Notice the word [Melan]esia with the root word melan as in melanin.

APPENDIX 11 CONTINUED:
"BLACK" MONGOLS

Here is a picture of melaninated Mongolian from 1260 to 1294 c.e. The first settlers of the land dates back to the migration of Homo Sapien-Sapiens leaving Africa around 60,000 b.c.e. These phenotype resemble the San people of Southern Africa.

APPENDIX 11 CONTINUED
HAWAIIANS

Kamehameha I (1810-1819)

Kamehameha I was the ruler of Hawaii prior to European colonialization. He was the first king of Hawaii establishing a dynasty. Kamehameha was a talented warrior descendent from chiefs from Maui. He had several wives and the people of Hawaii claim their origins come from Africa.

APPENDIX 12

CRISPUS ATTUCKS NATIVE AMERICAN

Speculative 19th century portrait of Crispus Attucks

Crispus Attucks (c.1723—March 5, 1770) was the first casualty of the Boston massacre, in Boston, Massachusetts, and is widely considered to be the first American casualty in the American Revolutionary War. Aside from the event of his death, along with Samuel Gray and James Caldwell, little is known for certain about Attucks. He may have been an African American slave or freeman, merchant seaman and dockworker of **Wampanoag** and African descent. His father was an African-born slave and his mother a **Native American.**

APPENDIX 13

INDIGENOUS HOLIDAYS: SUN DANCE

The Sun Dance is a ceremony practiced differently by several North American Indigenous and Native Nations but many ceremonies have features in common including dancing, singing and drumming, the experience of visions, fasting and self torture.

APPENDIX 14

MOORISH SCIENCE

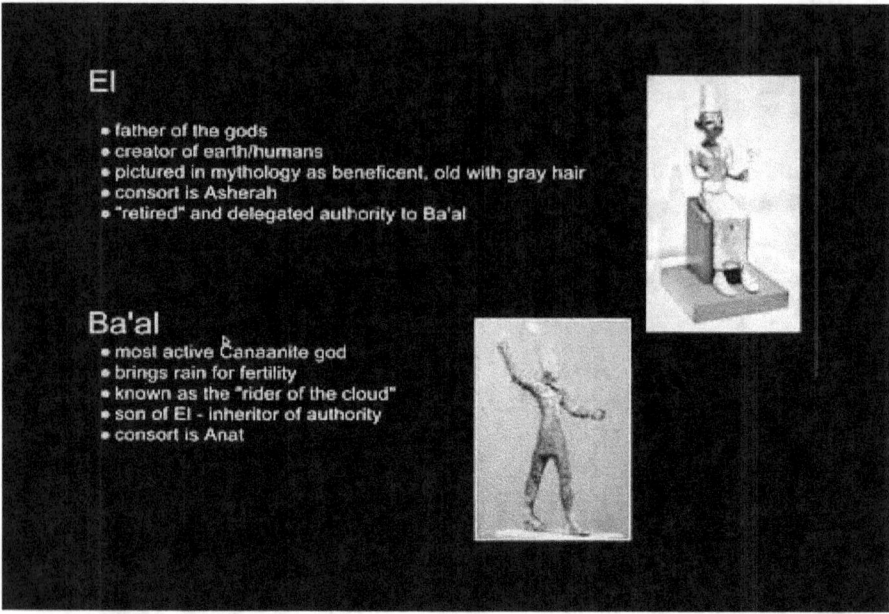

This demonstrates the surnames of Moorish people have their origins in Canaan. This is why Noble Drew Ali used these names to attach melaninated people back to the creed of their ancient for fathers/mothers. The title of Islamism [Old Time Religion] is really Canaanite and other ancient spiritual systems.

APPENDIX 15

ORISHAS AND SAINTS

Orisha	Saint	Principle
Agayu	Christopher	fatherhood
Babaluaye	Lazarus	illness
Eleggua	Nino de Atocha, Anthony of Padua	way-opener, messenger, trickster
Ibeji (twins)	Cosmus and Damien	children
Inle	Rafael	medicine
Obatala	Mercedes	clarity
Ogun	Peter	iron
Olokun	Regla	profundity
Orula	Francis	wisdom, destiny
Osanyin	Joseph	herbs
Oshosi	Norbert	hunt, protection
Oshun	Caridad	eros, rivers
Oya	Candelaria	death
Shango	Barbara	force, thunder
Yemaya	Regla	maternity, seas

The religion of the West African Yoruba people was forced underground by centuries of slavery in the Americas. Several hybrid forms of worship, of which the best known is Santeria, were created by deliberate conflation of Yoruba spiritual entities with Catholic ones.

APPENDIX 16

DIVINATION

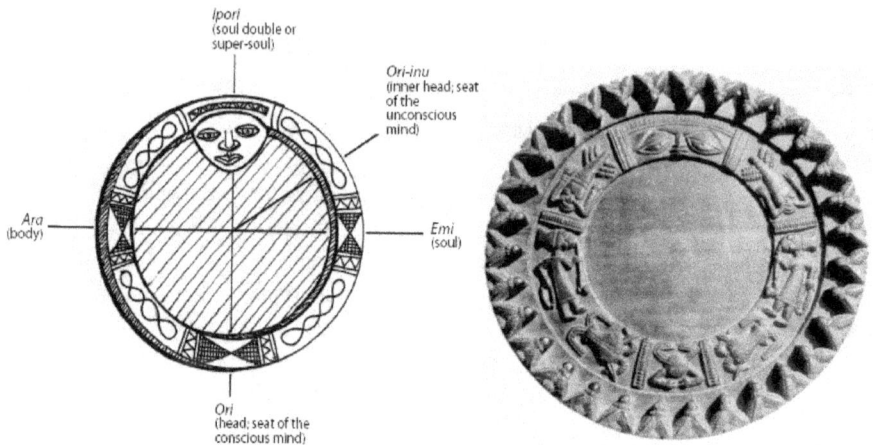

These are trays used by a Yoruba priest or diviner, Babalawo. Yoruba Ifa oracle trays are marked by the head of Esu, which is positioned opposite the diviner. The tray is fed annually by the members of a secret society. During this act of feeding, it gives increased Ase (power) to the diviner and increases the power of their divination. Below is a picture of cowery shells used in divination.

APPENDIX 17

ALTARS/SHRINES

This is an Ancestral shrine/altar in a typical African setting. It is very important to clean and cleanse the area. Frankincense, myrrh and Sage are used to purify the area from any negative or dark energies or spirits. Make sure the area is neat and clear to attract order instead of chaotic energy.

APPENDIX 18
ANCESTOR MONEY

Ancestral money is use mostly at funerals. The burning of the money allows for the object to be transferred to ancestors or ghost materializing in the afterlife. The social and non-religious function of ancestor worship is to cultivate kinship values like family loyalty and continunity of the family lineage. When burning ghost money, the sheets are treated as real money and not casually tossed into a fire but placed gently into a loose bundle.

APPENDIX 19
POLYGAMY

2. HISTORICAL BACKGROUND OF POLYGAMY.

- Islam did not invent the system of polygamy. It existed long before Islam came into the scene of world events.

- Many holy personalities of the Bible had many wives or concubines at the same time.

- Abraham had Sarah and Hajar. Abraham was first blessed with a son through Hajar whom he named Ishmael, and then he was blessed with another son through Sarah whom he named Isaac.

- Look at the example of Jacob; he had four wives and concubines: Leah and Rachel (both were Jacob's cousins), and he also had Bilhah and Zilpah (both were slave-girls gifted to Jacob by his wives). It is from these four ladies that Jacob had twelve sons who became ancestors of the Twelve Tribes of Israel.

- David, known in Arabic as Prophet Dawūd, had at least eight wives whose names are known and he had many others whose names have not been recorded.

BIBLICAL REFEERENCES TO POLYGAMY

APPENDIX 19:
CONTINUED POLYGAMY

COUNTRIES/REGIONS WHERE POLYGAMY IS LEGAL		
Afghanistan	The Gambia	Pakistan
Algeria	India	Palestine
Bahrain	Indonesia	Qatar
Bangladesh	Iran	Saudi Arabia
Brunei	Iraq	Senegal
Burkina Faso	Jordan	Singapore
Cameroon	Kuwait	Somalia
Chad	Libya	Sri Lanka
CAR	Malaysia	Sudan
Comoros	Maldives	Syria
Congo	Mali	Tanzania
Djibouti	Mauritania	Togo
Egypt	Morocco	Uganda
Ethiopia	Myanmar	UAW
Gabon	Niger	Yemen
	Oman	Zambia

APPENDIX 20:
INDIGENOUS FOODS

The secret is out: 10 African super foods you need to be eating and drinking right now

From teff, moringa, amaranth and hibiscus, here's some health secrets of Africa's most nutritious plants

THE number of hungry people in the world has dropped to 795 million from 1 billion in 1990-92, to the latest State of Food Insecurity in the World 2015 (SOFI).

Released in Rome on May 27, SOFI 2015 reported that in the developing regions, the prevalence of undernourishment declined to 12.9% of the population, down from 23.3% a quarter century ago.

The report published by the UN's Food and Agriculture Organisation (FAO), the International Fund for Agricultural Development (IFAD) and the World Food Programme (WFP) praised the efforts of Africa, in particular western Africa, in achieving their millennium development goals (MDG) hunger target.

However, despite the progress, sub-Saharan Africa is the region with the highest prevalence of undernourishment in the world, at 23.2%.

The situation could get better - or worse - depending on how the continent's and the world's love affairs with some of its increasingly popular foods plays out.

Early this month, the Ethiopian government announced plans to allow the partial lifting of a ban on exports of teff grain, touted as the newest "superfood" in the health food circuits particularly in the Europe and North America.

But the challenge will be how to get high prices internationally while keeping prices low locally, to avoid the fate that befell other "super foods" like quinoa and spelt that became too expensive for ordinary farmers in the end.

Under the plan, Ethiopian teff will be produced commercially for export under tight government control on 48 farms throughout the country, according to a report in GeeskaAfrika.

We look at 10 super foods in Africa that pack a serious nutritional punch, that you should be eating - and drinking - right now:

1. Teff

Grown predominantly in Ethiopia and Eritrea, teff is a fine grain that packs a serious nutritional punch. It leads all the grains – by a large margin – in its calcium content, with a cup of cooked teff containing 123mg of calcium, about the same as half a cup of spinach. It's also high in protein, iron, and – unusual for a grain – in vitamin C.

Used to make the traditional flatbread injera which is a regional stable, export of teff grain or flour have been banned by the Ethiopian government since 2006.

No doubt the Ethiopian government has looked nervously at the example of another superfood, quinoa, which has become so popular on the global stage that many people in its native countries - Peru and Bolivia - can no longer afford to buy it. And hunger is a political issue in Ethiopia that the authorities have an extremely low tolerance for.

2. Fonio

Native to the West African Sahel, fonio is a drought-resistant grain related to millet, that is high in amino acids and is a favourite in salads, stews and porridges.

Like teff, fonio matures quickly, producing grain in just six to eight weeks, and so can be relied upon in semi-arid areas with poor soil and unreliable rainfall.

It's rising in popularity among foodies in big cities like New York, but there are also concerns that although large scale fonio exports would be profitable for local farmers, they themselves could end up being priced out of the market.

3. Amaranth

Known by various names in Africa – mchicha in Swahili, terere among the Gikuyu, Meru and Embu of Kenya, doodo in Uganda and shoko in Yoruba, both the leaves and grain of amaranth are used as food.

Amaranth grain contains about 30% more protein than cereals like rice, sorghum and rye; its nutritional profile is comparable to wheat germ and oats

Compared to other grains, amaranth is unusually rich in the essential amino acid lysine. Common grains such as wheat and corn are comparatively rich in amino acids that amaranth lacks; thus, amaranth and grains can complement each other.

4. Moringa

If you can disguise the heavy chlorophyll taste, moringa oleifera gives you one of the most nutrient-dense packages around.

Native to Africa and South Asia, all parts of the moringa tree – bark, pods, leaves, nuts, seeds, tubers, roots, and flowers – are edible.

The leaves are used fresh or dried and ground into powder, and are high in protein, calcium, iron, Vitamin C and Vitamin A; some estimates show that gram-for-gram, moringa contains twice the protein of yoghurt, four times the calcium of milk, seven times the Vitamin C of oranges and 25 times the iron of spinach.

Advocacy groups are now touting moringa as a remedy for malnutrition in Africa, especially among infants, children and nursing mothers.

Moringa is especially promising as a food source in the tropics because the tree is in full leaf at the end of the dry season when other foods are typically scarce.

5. Pumpkin leaves

Commonly known in Nigeria as "ugwu/ ugu", pumpkin leaves are eaten all over Africa and form a common part of the diet when available; leaves can be eaten fresh or dried.

They can be steamed like spinach, sauteed in some olive oil with garlic and salt, or used in stir frys and stews.

Pumpkin leaves contain a healthy amount of Vitamin A, Vitamin C, calcium, and iron, as well as folate, potassium, and some of the B-vitamins.

6. Baobab fruit

The iconic baobab is a common tree in eastern and southern Africa's savannahs, and its fruit provides nutrition to both humans and many other animals, from birds to honey bees.

Baobab fruit is very dry so it keeps almost indefinitely, and it is used to make juice from its powder of by soaking the fruit and straining out the pulp and seeds.

Baobab fruit is particularly high in antioxidants, as well as fibre (10 times the fibre of apples), potassium, magnesium and iron.

Powdered baobab leaves are commonly sold in markets around West Africa, and can be mixed in to juices and smoothies.

7. Hibiscus

Hibiscus tea at a café in Aswan, Egypt.

When dried hibiscus flowers are steeped in hot water, the dark red hibiscus tea is called karkadeh/ karkady in Arabic, and is popular in North Africa, particularly Egypt and Sudan. In Egypt and Sudan, wedding celebrations are traditionally toasted with a glass of hibiscus tea.

In West Africa, it's known as bissap, tsoborodo or wonjo; bissap is called the "national drink of Senegal." Hibiscus tea is rich in antioxidants minerals and vitamin C, and served hot it loses a bit of its characteristic sour. It can also be served chilled with ice.

8. Tamarind

Native to tropical Africa and prized for its sweet-and-sour flavour, tamarind (also known as ukwaju in Swahili) is used to make juice, and is rich in vitamins, minerals and antioxidants.

Its sticky pulp is a rich source of dietary fibre; 100 g of fruit pulp provides 5.1 or over 13% of the dietary fibre that you typically need in a day.

Tamarind is particularly useful for restoring electrolyte imbalance when you're experiencing dehydration, which is why many East African coastal communities will serve a glass of ukwaju to a guest coming in from a hot day – or as a hangover remedy.

9. Coconut

The humble coconut, ubiquitous to tropical coastlines everywhere, has some serious health benefits. Its unique fatty-acid combination promotes healthy brain function; protein-containing coconut milk aids the digestive system, is a natural antiviral, and boosts skin health.

Like tamarind, coconut water is a great electrolytic drink, rehydrating the body at a cellular level.

10. Kenkiliba

The leaves from Kenkiliba shrub, native to the Sahel, are used to make an infusion tea that is touted as a digestive detoxifier and cure-all, common in Burkina Faso, Mali, Senegal, Guinea and the Gambia.

Some West African Muslims will break their all-day Ramadhan fast with bread and a sweet and milky kenkiliba tea, as kenkiliba is a digestive stimulant.

OTHER BOOKS BY BANDELE EL AMIN

www.ingramcontent.com/pod-product-compliance
Lightning Source LLC
Chambersburg PA
CBHW072124280526

45788CB00002B/528